THIRTY-ONE DAILY REA
BE GOSPEL-SATURATED A

goSpeL
MEDiTATIONS
for
MISSIONS

CHRIS ANDERSON

JD CROWLEY

DAVID HOSAFLOOK

TIM KEESEE

JOE TYRPAK

INTRODUCTION

I've often thought of myself as an observer of Christian missions. As a child, a college student, and finally a pastor, I appreciated commando-type Christians who took the Gospel to unreached places. But I didn't think of it as normal Christianity—and certainly not as a part of my life.

I was wrong. Missions is a normal part of every Christian's life. Over the last several years, the Lord has graciously and relentlessly opened my eyes to the Bible's almost constant missionary emphasis. He's used sermons. He's used books like Piper's *Let the Nations Be Glad*, Doran and Johnson's *For the Sake of His Name*, Platt's *Radical*, Peters' *A Biblical Theology of Missions*, and numerous biographies. He's used the highly-acclaimed video series *Dispatches from the Front* by Tim Keesee. He's used real-life missionaries, including those supported by my church, my brother Dan (director of Brazil Gospel Fellowship Mission), my father-in-law Jack Leeds (who retired early to go to the field), JD Crowley, and David Hosaflook—all modern missionary heroes. Most of all, He's used the Scriptures to show me the "normalcy" of missions.

Christians must be confronted with missions on a regular, even daily basis. It's toward that end that we publish *Gospel Meditations for Missions*. I pray they will inform and inspire college students, church members, pastors, and even missionaries for the grand cause of world evangelization. As with *Gospel Meditations for Men* and *Gospel Meditations for Women*, I urge you to immerse yourself in the Scriptures prior to studying our comments. As you read the book, capture the passion of the writers, especially those who write *about* the mission field *from* the mission field. And respond with prayerful, audacious obedience: "Here am I, Lord. Send me."

For the sake of His name,

Chris Anderson, *editor*

Chris Anderson is the founding pastor of Tri-County Bible Church in Madison, Ohio. He is the founder of *churchworksmedia.com*, where he has published hymns (including "His Robes for Mine" and "For the Sake of His Name") and the *Gospel Meditations* series of devotionals.

JD Crowley has lived in Asian cultures all his life. After 12 years of pastoring in Hawaii, he went to Cambodia in 1994 to do linguistic and mission work among the indigenous minorities there. He is the author of *The Tampuan/Khmer/English Dictionary* and Khmer commentaries on Matthew and Romans.

David Hosaflook went to Albania in 1992 on a short-term mission trip. Almost two decades later, he's still there, helping to evangelize people and plant churches in the wake of what was the most oppressive communist regime in eastern Europe. He loves Albanian history and will soon publish *The Siege of Shkodra*, a work on the Ottoman/Christian struggle in Albania.

Tim Keesee is the director of Frontline Missions International, an organization committed to advancing the Gospel in the world's difficult places by developing sustainable platforms for work and witness. He is the executive producer of the missions documentary series *Dispatches from the Front*. He has authored numerous books and articles on history, politics, and missions.

Joe Tyrpak is the assistant pastor at Tri-County Bible Church. He is a gifted artist (responsible for this book's design) and an insightful teacher. He has composed several metrical psalms and co-authored the *Gospel Meditations* series, all available from *churchworksmedia.com*.

© 2011 by churchworksmedia.com. All rights reserved.

Scripture quotations on Days 2, 9, 14, 21, 24, and 31 are from the *King James Version*.
All other quotations are from *The Holy Bible, English Standard Version*, copyright © 2001 by Crossway Bibles, a division of Good News Publishers. Used by permission. All rights reserved.

GOD IS THE GREAT MISSIONARY

For the Father is seeking such people to worship him. JOHN 4:23

Missions isn't an addendum that was stapled onto normal Christianity. It's at the heart of Christianity because it's at the heart of God Himself. God is the Great Missionary of the Scriptures. We see His missionary heart from the beginning of time, when He sought out our lost and evasive parents in Eden. We see it when He promised Abraham that all the nations of the world will be blessed through his (and His) seed. We see it when He promised to make the Messiah the King of an unending Kingdom and the Light of the darkened Gentiles. We certainly see it in John 4. Jesus' interaction with the spiritually thirsty woman at the well is a microcosm of God's work in the world. Again and again through the conversation with her, with the disciples, and with a village of Samaritan converts, God's heart for missions is shown in all its glory.

The Great Missionary is seeking worshipers. In the middle of His discussion with the Samaritan woman, Jesus makes a startling and apparently random comment in verse 23: "The Father is seeking ... people to worship Him." That's one of the most important statements in Scripture. *God is seeking worshipers.* It's amazing. It's life-shaping. It's the plotline of the whole Bible. God *made* us for His glory. Though we rebelled, God planned to *save* us for His glory, and He carried out that plan through the incarnation, life, death, and resurrection of His Son. God is the Great Missionary. He's not distant and ambivalent, perhaps willing to forgive sinners should we decide to seek after Him. On the contrary, He's the *Planner* of salvation. The *Initiator*. The *Accomplisher*. The *Goal*. In the memorable first words of John Piper's *Let the Nations Be Glad*, "Missions exists because worship doesn't." God is seeking worshipers in order to display His glorious grace (Ephesians 1:6, 12, 14).

The Great Missionary is making worshipers. Here's the thing. When God looks throughout the earth, He doesn't find a bunch of good-hearted people just waiting to be assembled into a heavenly choir. Rather, He finds rebels. He sees only our backs as we defiantly run our own way (Isaiah 53:6; Romans 3:10-11). Yes, God is seeking worshipers, but He doesn't *find* them. He *makes* them! From what? From Samaritan women, for starters! From sinners like us. That's why the context of John 4:23 is so crucial. The statement that God is seeking people to worship Him in spirit and in truth isn't coming in a treatise about music or liturgy. It's coming in the midst of one of the great evangelistic conversations in history. Jesus is telling a disreputable and broken woman that God is seeking worshipers—and making them out of people like her! The location of worship (about which she had asked in 4:20) wasn't the issue. Her sinful past wasn't the issue (4:16-19). Faith in Him as the saving Messiah was (4:25-26). Thus, God is seeking *worshipers* (4:23) as Jesus seeks and saves *the lost* (Luke 19:10). Those two statements are essentially the same!

The Great Missionary is calling us into His great missionary work. Christ's agenda included much more than this unnamed Samaritan woman. In His missionary zeal, He next focused on His disciples, urging them to emulate His missionary heart (4:27-38). Though all they could see in the Samaritan people was rivalry and race, Jesus told them to open their eyes and see a spiritual harvest (4:35). An entire village of lost people was in the process of becoming worshipers of "the Savior of the world" (4:42). The disciples needed to get with Christ's program. They needed to learn the joy of doing the Father's will—*missions* (4:34). They needed to pray for laborers who would participate with God in the execution of His eternal, doxological rescue mission. They needed to devote their lives to bringing that harvest in. And they would. Will you?

Let the Gospel open your eyes to the harvest of worshipers around the world. —CHRIS

Is Your Spirit Stirred?

While Paul waited for them at Athens, his spirit was stirred. ACTS 17:16

In Acts 17 Paul, Silas, and Timothy are in Thessalonica facing heavy persecution from a rabble gang thrown together by antagonistic Jews (v. 5). At night, some concerned brothers smuggle the small squad away to the nearby town of Berea (v. 10). There the team does what it always did: it finds people to tell about Jesus. The Bereans turn out to be a hungry-hearted, Scripture-searching bunch (v. 11). But for the Thessalonian Jews, Berea is threateningly close, so they mobilize their mob to unleash mayhem there, too (v. 13). Again some brothers whisk Paul away, this time to Athens, but for some reason—probably logistical—Silas and Timothy get left behind (v. 14). (Sorry, fellas.)

Now Paul finds himself alone in Athens, waiting for his team to rejoin him. What a perfect chance for some "down time," for sightseeing or finding an Internet café to tweet about the *tzatziki*. Can you imagine Paul's social networking update? "Whew! Back-to-back escapes. Those Thessalonians have *issues*."

Don't think so. Paul's only notion of "working a net" was fishing for souls—preaching Christ and Him crucified (1 Corinthians 1:23, Galatians 6:14). Yes, he saw some sights in Athens, but everything he saw was filtered through his worldview as a man crucified with Christ (Galatians 2:20). Mysteriously and magnificently, Christ was "in him" (Colossians 1:27-29), so he grew to love what Christ loves and lament what Christ laments. When Paul "saw the city wholly given to idolatry," something both awful and wonderful happened within him. *His spirit was stirred* (v. 16). His gut was wrenched. A lump of grief knotted his throat. A surge of holy jealousy flushed his face because God—*his* God, the only *true* God—was being ... *maligned?* ... No, that wasn't it .... *Rejected?* ... No, that wasn't quite it either. Alas, his God was ... totally ... *unknown* (v. 23)!

The lump in Paul's throat swiftly morphed into a leap in his step. See him at the synagogue engaging the potential Jehovah-fearers (v. 17a). Now he's in the marketplace preaching—and will be there tomorrow, and the next day, and the next (v. 17b). His message is gaining steam (v. 18). He's now heading to Athens' Supreme Court, the Areopagus, which once met on the hill of the Greek god Ares—Mars Hill (v. 19). Paul's adrenalin must be surging now. He's a volcano ready to erupt. Go, Paul! Knock Ares & Friends off their pedestals, for Jesus is King of the hill, Supreme Justice of the world!

Paul's spiritual psychology is instructive. He's not a reluctant "missionary" on assignment. He's what I call a "passionary." There's a huge difference between mission and passion. Mission is required; passion is acquired. Mission is duty; passion is delight. Mission says, "I *have to* witness"; passion says, "I *get to* witness!" If all you have is mission, that's okay—It's not hypocrisy to obey orders despite a deficiency of passion. But the more you "mish," the more you will acquire the inner fire that Paul showed in Athens.

Soon after I arrived in Albania, I was begging God to help me love as He loves and grieve as He grieves. A *muezzin* began to howl from one of our city's many mosques. Then another. And another. The cacophony was beckoning thousands to embrace a faith that cannot save. Most tourists think "the call to prayer" is novel and culturally inspiring. But tears were streaming down my face. Why? Because God's compassion had come to my breast. You know of what I speak. You have felt powerful pangs of compassion for your hurting neighbors, for sinning co-workers, and for lost tribes in faraway lands. Those are passionary pangs. God put them in your heart. He is stirring your spirit.

Meditating on missions is meaningless without movement. When God stirs your spirit, He also loosens your tongue, rattles your routine, and gets you off the couch.

Let the Gospel stir you—inside and out. —DAVID

ONE-WAY TICKET

On frequent journeys, in danger from rivers, danger from robbers, danger from my own people, danger from Gentiles, danger in the city, danger in the wilderness, danger at sea, danger from false brothers. 2 CORINTHIANS 11:26

Paul wrote half of the New Testament, but he never wrote his memoirs. We have only a few pages in Luke's history about Paul's thirty years of breath-taking, back-breaking, nation-shaking Gospel ministry, and even fewer tantalizing lines from Paul's own pen: "danger from rivers, danger from robbers, danger…, danger…, danger" (2 Corinthians 11:26). The fact is, the struggles and soldiering of Kingdom-work are mostly done in obscurity. In many parts of the world today believers labor and suffer in silence—Years in prison or a refugee camp pass unnoticed by the outside world. Nothing on Google, no biographies, no blogs. The viewpoint of most everyone around them is that these Christians are fools who have wasted their lives on a lost cause. This is nothing new—From the first century and the first martyrs who were burned to ash or became the food of wild beasts to the 21st century and Christians who suffer in silence or slog through nameless, indifferent places for the Gospel, great sacrifice has often gone unnoticed.

During a trip in southern Egypt I came across an old Christian cemetery where a number of missionaries had been buried long ago. The desert heat shimmered over a scattering of crumbling mud-brick markers and broken epitaphs. It was so desolate. I thought of these men and women setting out for the field. They must have parted from their families with kisses and tears, but also with the joy that rushes the heart when Jesus is near. They followed Christ across the Atlantic to tell people about their Friend and Savior. They crossed the ocean but never re-crossed it. For them, missionary service was a one-way ticket. Of course, cross-bearing is a one-way ticket, too.

Jesus Himself reminded us of the beauty of extravagant service just days before Gethsemane and Calvary. As Jesus dined with His followers, a woman came and broke open a costly flask of fragrant spikenard and poured it without reservation upon the head of the Lord (Matthew 26:6-13). He knew that in just a few days His head would be torn with thorns and that the hair that now glistened with fragrant oil would soon be matted with blood and spit. Somehow, perhaps because she had been listening more closely than others, Mary knew, too. To their shame, it was the disciples who shook their heads and said, "Why this waste" (26:8)? Sometimes the strongest and most hurtful opposition to this kind of lavish, loving, risk-taking abandonment comes from other Christians. But Jesus said, "Why do you trouble the woman, for she has done a beautiful thing to me" (26:10). These words speak peace and purpose over that old Egyptian graveyard and over those I love—brothers and sisters who walk lonely paths in His service.

Much of the world remains unreached. If we look at statistics, listen to the voices of unbelief in our own ranks, or focus on our fears, then the cause seems lost and the effort too risky. But Christ has simply told us, "Follow me." And for those with a heart for Him, He will lead them through impossibilities as He builds His Kingdom in every land. Pray for men and women with such hearts to follow Him there. Pray that you would follow Him there, too.

Let the Gospel comfort and compel you, even when no one seems to care. —TIM

AN OVERLOOKED MISSIONS HYMN

Why do the nations rage and the peoples plot in vain? PSALM 2:1

What are the most encouraging missionary hymns you can think of? Among the several you might list, I can almost guarantee that you wouldn't include the favorite missionary hymn of the early church: Psalm 2.

The second psalm is a God-breathed coronation hymn. Its first stanza considers how world rulers are constantly plotting to *subvert* God's chosen king (vv. 1-3). The second and third stanzas reflect on the Lord's calm *sovereignty* (vv. 4-6) as He reaffirms His invincible plan to *subjugate* every nation under His anointed king (vv. 7-9). In the final stanza, the Lord advises every king in the world to *submit* to His anointed (vv. 10-12). The people of Israel probably sang the four verses of this anthem at the enthronement of every king. It reminded them that their king was God's anointed and that no enemy could overthrow his reign (as long as the king remained faithful to God's law). Even more significantly, this hymn ultimately applies to Israel's greatest Son of David, Jesus *the* Anointed, the King of kings whose reign would never end. These are grand themes, and they have missionary implications, as the fledgling church in Acts demonstrates.

This hymn comforts us in persecution. Peter and John were imprisoned for preaching the Gospel (Acts 3:1-4:4). As soon as the Sanhedrin released them from jail, they met with the church in Jerusalem. In the heat of the moment, the early church spontaneously prayed Psalm 2:1-2, word-for-word, as a group (Acts 4:24-26). It's not likely that they all had their Bibles open in front of them. (The printing press hadn't been invented yet.) Instead, they knew it from memory, probably because they had studied, sung, and prayed it so frequently. They had enjoyed the healing of this balm before. For them, persecution wasn't rare, and this persecution wasn't the worst. The worst raging of the Gentiles against God's Anointed King had taken place at the crucifixion. The cross was simultaneously the most heinous sin in human history and the climactic event in God's sovereign plan for history (4:27-28). As we remember that God ruled amidst the injustice and bloodshed at Calvary, we'll find His comfort amidst our own suffering for the Gospel—the comfort Psalm 2 intends to give.

This hymn emboldens us for proclamation. As the early church reflected on the truths of Psalm 2, they prayed not for safety or political change, but for boldness in the face of certain opposition (4:29-31). The early church had "chewed on" Psalm 2 long enough to become convinced that it provided them with the right to proclaim the Gospel to every culture. Because Jesus is God's Anointed, the universal King, believers have His authority as His ambassadors to spread the news of His reign so that people from every nation will submit to Him.

There is immense comfort here for us! How it inspires our confidence in the Lord! We don't have to fear people or their reactions! This inspired anthem should continue to be central in our prayers for the Gospel's advance. We, like the early church, should know it by heart, sing it often, and experience its power to comfort and embolden our Gospel endeavors.

Let the Gospel prompt your prayer for its bold proclamation amidst opposition. —JOE

WHAT ACTS 1:8 REALLY MEANS

But you will receive power when the Holy Spirit has come upon you, and you will be my witnesses in Jerusalem and in all Judea.... ACTS 1:8

Sometimes an interpretation that's popular in Christian culture hijacks the intended meaning of a text. Take Acts 1:8. Do a web search on it and almost all the hits will say something like "Where is your Jerusalem? Where is your Samaria?"—as if the main point of the verse is that every church down through the centuries has to become "Jerusalem" and repeat the steps that the first church took. If all we're thinking about when we read Acts 1:8 is "Where is *our* Jerusalem?" we're subjectivizing objective truth (It's all about us, isn't it!), and missing something really, really huge that Jesus is doing.

So what's the huge thing Jesus is doing? He's using a multi-dimensional approach to prophecy that the apostles would have recognized from the Old Testament. Israel's prophets often gave both a short-term and long-term prediction. If the short-term prediction fizzled, no need to wait around for the long-term prediction; the guy was a false prophet. But if the short-term prediction happened, the rest was guaranteed.

Jesus is doing the same thing in Acts 1:8. The disciples need some serious encouragement. In a few minutes the Lord will leave, and they'll have to go back to the city that's famous for killing prophets (Matthew 23:37). What final words will Jesus leave with them? This is not the time for a missions strategy pep talk about reaching "*your* Jerusalem and *your* Samaria." It's time for the most audacious short-term and long-term predictions that a prophet ever gave.

"But you will receive power when the Holy Spirit has come upon you." The Holy Spirit is the key to everything that follows. Do you really think the scaredy-cat apostles are going to turn Jerusalem upside down without the boldness of the Spirit? Or reach across that impossible chasm to the hated Samaritans without the love of the Spirit? Or make God famous to the ends of the earth without the endurance of the Spirit? The Holy Spirit of God is the only engine that can power this stunning drive to the very last people group. And He's the only One who can keep it all from flying apart.

If this new thing called "the church" is going to take over the world with the Gospel, the Holy Spirit isn't going to do the same thing He did in the Old Testament. In the Old Testament it was "Come and see." "Come, Naaman. Come, Queen of Sheba. Come to Israel where God's Spirit-filled prophets are preaching. Come to Jerusalem where God's Spirit-filled priests are ministering in God's temple." But Jesus inaugurated the new age of Holy Spirit power. It's no longer "Come and see," but "Go and tell." Every city becomes the holy city; every people becomes the chosen people; every church and every believer become the holy temple.

What if this first prediction had fizzled? End of story. Game over. Jesus is a false prophet. But it didn't fizzle—It *exploded*. The Spirit came in power! Check it off the list.

"You will be my witnesses in Jerusalem, and in all Judea." Hear this prediction through the ears of the apostles, and you'll see how impossible it sounds. Humanly speaking, the mission to reach Jerusalem should have ended with eleven more crosses on Golgotha. Yet here was the risen Lord telling them that they wouldn't get snuffed out. They would successfully make Jesus famous in Jerusalem and Judea.

Well, did it happen? I need to know. Because if it didn't, I'm checking out. I'm not waiting around. I'll go and find a savior I can trust. But it *did* happen, and it happened in a big way. Three thousand people in one day. Five thousand more a little while later. Glory! Check it off the list. Two down, two to go. (Continued tomorrow.)

Let the Gospel blow you away with its audacious promises. —JD

CHECK IT OFF THE LIST

...You will be my witnesses in Jerusalem and in all Judea and Samaria, and to the end of the earth. ACTS 1:8

We would never teach the account of the crucifixion and then immediately ask, "What is *your* Calvary?" As important as it is for us to follow the example of Calvary, it's not even one millionth as important as what Christ *did* on Calvary. Yet that's often how Acts 1:8 is handled. The "Where is *our* Jerusalem, *our* Judea, *our* Samaria?" paradigm has muted the main purpose of the text, which is to authenticate the prophetic status of the Lord Jesus, to predict the glorious victories of the Gospel, and to provide strong encouragement for the church. We saw yesterday that Christ nailed the first two predictions about the coming of the Holy Spirit and the evangelization of Jerusalem and Judea. We can check those off the list.

Don't think that "check those off the list" means that we don't have to go back and evangelize Jerusalem again. Of course, every generation needs the Gospel. I mean "check it off the *prophecy* list." If Christ can't get the short-term predictions right, no sense waiting around for the others. But He did get them right, which brings us to audacious predictions 3 and 4.

"You will be my witnesses ... in Samaria." Samaria? The disciples had just asked the Lord about when He was going to restore *Israel* (1:6), and now He's talking about Samaria? If the thought of evangelizing Jerusalem was scary, evangelizing Samaria was just plain disgusting. "Lord, they're not like us." Do you see that this third prediction is nothing less than a promise that the Gospel of Jesus Christ will plunge a cross-shaped dagger right into the heart of racism? According to the book of Ephesians, a colorful church is a testimony to the whole world (seen and unseen) that the cross has power to tear down racial walls that have been standing for hundreds and even thousands of years (Ephesians 2–3). In Acts 8 the walls started tumbling.

So where are we on our checklist? The Holy Spirit would come powerfully and inaugurate the new age. Check. The city and nation that killed Jesus would be reached for Christ. Check. The once-hated Samaritans would be brought into God's family through the Gospel. Check. And finally ...

"You will be my witnesses ... to the end of the earth." Can we check it off? Well, yes, we might as well, because we know from the fulfillment of the short-term predictions that this final long-term prophecy will come to pass without fail. But, no, the Gospel hasn't yet gone to the very *last* tribe and tongue and people group, though we know it will.

One of the problems with the "What is *our* Jerusalem" paradigm is that, if we keep thinking of our own city as Jerusalem, we fail to see the breathtaking fact that *our* churches are part of the fulfillment of this final prediction! When the Lord spoke these prophecies, few places on earth were more remote than Berryville, Virginia; Norman, Oklahoma; and Hilo, Hawaii. These places defined "the end of the earth." Hawaii wasn't even inhabited back then. Yet all these places and thousands in between have churches where God is worshiped through Christ by the power of the Holy Spirit!

So what? What does all this short-term/long-term stuff mean anyway? Just that Jesus is Lord! That God is real! That the Bible is trustworthy! That the Gospel is powerful! That every tribe and nation will come to Christ! That Jesus will return!

That's all.

Let the Gospel's past victories inspire present and future faith. —JD

THE GREAT COMMISSION[S]

As the Father has sent me, even so I am sending you. JOHN 20:21

I drive a Kia Soul. Don't judge me. And don't call it cute. I get that enough, and it's embarrassing. My point in mentioning my car is this: now that I'm driving one, I'm seeing Kias all over the place. They've been ubiquitous for quite a while; I just hadn't noticed. It strikes me that the topic of missions is that way in Scripture. It's everywhere, if you're paying attention. Robert Hall Glover writes: "The New Testament is uniquely and preeminently missionary—the greatest missionary volume ever produced. Every section of it was written by a missionary, with the primary object of meeting a missionary need and promoting missionary work" (*The Bible Basis for Missions*, p. 22). Of course, the high water mark of Scripture's focus on missions is the Great Commission—or, more accurately, Great Commissions (plural). Our resurrected Lord culminated His time on earth with four complementary missionary assignments.

Matthew 28:18-20 focuses on the universal authority of Christ. Jesus has the authority to issue this life-dominating, world-changing command. Why do Christians have the responsibility—and the audacity!—to take the Gospel of Jesus Christ across cultural and national boundaries? Because Jesus owns the earth. All authority in heaven and earth is His alone. Not only does He have the authority to issue the command; He has the authority to *accomplish* it. An otherwise impossible task is inevitable because an omnipotent hand is behind it. Thus, we go to make disciples of all nations, baptizing them to identify them as God's own possession and teaching them to obey Christ's commands. And the all-powerful Savior who sends us goes with us.

Mark 16:15-16 focuses on universal proclamation of the Gospel. Proclamation doesn't require a pulpit, nor is it primarily a preacher's task. Every Christian is a herald of the Gospel and is responsible to announce it boldly and authoritatively. The universality of the work is emphasized twice by Mark. Our task is all-encompassing *geographically* ("all the world") and *personally* ("every creature," KJV). We don't just take the Gospel to regions or nations, but to individuals, showing them that faith is the dividing line between forgiveness and condemnation (16:16).

Luke 24:46-48 focuses on the universal call to repentance. Twice in Luke 24, Christ roots His saving work in the Old Testament (24:25-27, 44-45). While I regret not hearing those lectures, I'm glad to have the Cliffs Notes in the New Testament epistles. Specifically, Christ told us that His death and resurrection were promised and necessary. To what end? That "repentance and forgiveness of sins should be proclaimed in his name to all nations." The tendency of many to excise repentance from the Gospel is a presumptuous perversion. Repentance was the message of John the Baptist (Matthew 3:2), of Jesus (Matthew 4:17), and of the apostles (Acts 2:38; 3:19). God calls *all people everywhere* to repent and turn to Christ (Acts 17:30). We are His witnesses, not filters.

John 20:21 focuses on the universal responsibility of believers. Throughout the book of John, we read again and again (almost forty times) that Jesus was sent by the Father (3:34; 5:23-24; et al.). He was, to quote Hebrews 3:1, the ultimate "Apostle" or "Sent One," and Christ entirely completed His mission (4:34; 17:4). It is staggering, then, that Jesus uses the same "sent" language when commissioning His church (17:18; 20:21). "As the Father has sent me, even so I am sending you." Jesus "deputized" the church to continue carrying out His mission of spiritual rescue, enabled by His Spirit (20:22; Luke 24:49). Christians, like Christ, have been sent into the world. Our orders couldn't be clearer. So what are we waiting for?

Let the Gospel be as urgent to you as it was to your Savior. —CHRIS

THE CROSS IS THE CENTER

So there will be one flock, one Shepherd. JOHN 10:16

There is a spot near the Temple of Heaven in Beijing, a little marble circle that marks what the ancient Chinese believed to be the very center of the universe. Today this cosmic bulls-eye is just a place for grinning tourists to stand and have their picture taken. In olden days, designating a particular place as the center of the universe was easy. But after a whole "new world" was discovered, little maps grew into great globes, and centers were more difficult to designate. Similarly, in the missions realm, our world is very different from the one in which William Carey, Adoniram Judson, and Hudson Taylor lived. Such missionary trailblazers inspired their generation to answer the Great Call. In the 19th and early 20th centuries, missionary ranks were filled mostly by people from the English-speaking world. But as they crossed continents and cultures with the Gospel, things changed. People of every nation, tongue, and tribe were saved through faith in Christ. Churches sprang up, and Christians around the world began sharing the Gospel with their own countrymen.

Contrary to our typical thinking, America is not the hub of God's missionary plan. The people God is using to advance the Gospel are very diverse—people who have strange names, speak in strange tongues, and eat strange foods. Unfortunately, when we talk about working with nationals—that is, Christians from other cultures and with differing experiences—we are often suspicious and concerned over accountability, and we differ in methods and practice. Such responses actually go back to the earliest days of the Church. As Acts unfolds, the "original" Christians (Jewish believers who thought Jerusalem was the center of the universe) grew concerned about the Gentile Christians. Some wanted to impose their Mosaic culture on these Greek and barbarian converts. The controversy (which Acts 15:2 describes as "no small dissension and debate") was so great that Paul and Barnabas had to come off the field and go to Jerusalem to address the situation. Eventually, Peter and the other leaders at Jerusalem wisely saw that the Gospel was about Christ and not preserving culture. Rather than imposing Jewish legal strictures on non-Jewish believers, they simply outlined a few simple requirements for Gentile believers for the purpose of purity and unity in the body of Christ. Then Paul and Barnabas got back to work!

This was not an isolated incident. "Cultural clashes" between Christians in the early Church are recorded throughout Acts and the epistles. So it's not surprising that there are misunderstandings among Christians today. The desire to impose cultural preferences along with the Gospel is just as real in the 21st century as it was in the first.

The need for unity isn't simply about "getting along with each other." It's about something so much bigger—It's about the cross. In Ephesians 2 we are reminded that Christ's work on the cross not only brings us into fellowship with the Father, but also into fellowship with all other believers. The most stunning—perhaps even uncomfortable—point Paul made to his initial, first-century audience was that there was no spiritual difference between two culturally different groups—Jewish believers and Gentile believers. Their cultural distinctions were deep and defining, but the significance of those differences was abolished by His death on the cross. Christ has made "one new man" (Ephesians 2:15). In the strongest possible terms, Paul pointed out that Christ was killed in order to "kill the hostility" (2:16). So then, what are *we* doing to kill the hostility? How are *we* showing love and respect for believers of different backgrounds? How do *we* reflect the radical Gospel truth that in all the world and for all time "there will be one flock, one Shepherd" (John 10:16)?

Let the Gospel free you to love Christians who are different from you. —TIM

ALL THINGS WORK TOGETHER FOR GOSPEL

The things which happened unto me have fallen out rather unto the furtherance of the gospel. PHILIPPIANS 1:12

Saint Paul—the consummate missionary. Lash him, and he bleeds with more passion to reach the lost. I would love to have been a fly on the tentflap in his strategy sessions with Barnabas or Silas. Certainly they must have pored over leathery maps and made use of a first-century equivalent of a yellow pad or whiteboard—brainstorming, networking, and making route plans for Gospel exploits.

But plans kept changing. There were obstacles. Like stonings. Team conflict. Traveling mobs. They knew they would face persecution, but never knew when, or where, or what, or from whom. Now Paul was in prison, writing to the Philippians. Though he had expected adversity, jail wasn't on this week's agenda. How did he respond?

He may have thought of Romans 8:28, which he had written several years previously. That verse prods us to acknowledge everything in our lives as orchestrated by our Father for good—indeed for *our* good. But we have come to misuse the text as a cliché: Whenever someone loses a job or has a fender bender, several church members are bound to quip, "All things work together!" Then they unwittingly butcher the application by asserting that God "must have a better job in store"; He "must have been protecting you from a worse crash down the road." That all may be true, but it's not the point of the verse.

Let's not cheapen Romans 8:28 by confining it to the temporal or making it all about us. God is at work in "all things" to conform us to the image of His Son (8:29). This inner transformation demands missional outflow, seeing that we are conforming to the One who is constantly seeking the lost. So in the dungeon, Paul's interpretation of "all things working together for good" was not some vague hope of a better situation in the future, nor a passive acknowledgment that someday he might understand the sovereign patchwork. Certainly there are millions of inscrutable purposes for each unexpected happening, but Paul focused and acted upon one explanation of which he was certain: God sends saved people to lost people, and He wants them to preach the Gospel.

He wrote, "The things which happened unto me have fallen out … unto the furtherance of the gospel" (Philippians 1:12). Eureka! A fleshing out of Romans 8:28! Paul shows us how to see and seize opportunities with confidence in God's control over events—not for a nebulous "good," but for the specific good of Gospel advance. It's like getting new eyes to see Gospel designs in our seasons of pain or frustration. In the middle of your affliction, with whom can you share Christ? The "good" God promises may be a lower-paying job with a lost coworker that He has been ripening for harvest. A Cornelius. An Ethiopian eunuch. A woman at the well. What if God is choosing you as His messenger, right now, right here? Your hardship is for God's glory. And for the coworker's good. And, if you love God, for your good, too.

The Romans 8:28 promise is for those "who love God." Those who do will grow to love what He loves—and He loves unfurling His glorious Gospel. Because God is ordering your steps, because He is on a grand campaign to draw people to Himself, and because He wants you to proclaim the Gospel, therefore, you can safely assume that the weird, painful, or frustrating thing that just happened must certainly have something to do with Gospel expansion. Is your antenna up?

God's yellow pad is smarter than yours. Detours provide new networks to spread the message of eternal joy. For Gospel-centered, God-loving people, what could be better?

Let the Gospel interpret your interruptions. —DAVID

JOPPA & THE GENTILES

To the Gentiles also God has granted repentance that leads to life.
ACTS 11:18

Joppa is a small port town on the Israeli Mediterranean coastline. Today it's overshadowed by Tel Aviv, Israel's modern playground. But throughout the centuries, Joppa has been a symbolic point of departure for world evangelization.

In the Old Testament, Joppa was the place of Gentile exclusion. Jonah 1:1 contains a momentous step forward in God's plan for the nations. Classic commentator Hugh Martin calls it "a golden and indispensable link in the onward movement of that great redemption." Throughout the Old Testament we read of the universal scope of redemption (Genesis 12:3; Isaiah 2:2-4). But Gentiles were welcomed on a limited basis. They had to come to Israel, as the Queen of Sheba did. Judaism's evangelistic message amounted to an invitation to "Come and see," not a command to "Go and tell." Furthermore, Gentiles essentially had to become Israelites to associate with Jehovah, as Ruth did. There was no "missionary movement" to the nations at large.

All of that began to change in Jonah 1:1. For the first time, God sent a prophet out of Palestine and to a pagan city—*the* pagan city. The prophet Jonah was less than enthused with God's commission to preach in Nineveh. It was the equivalent of asking a Jew to preach in Berlin in 1940. Fearful that God would spare the wicked Ninevites, Jonah—the Old Testament counterpart to the prodigal's "older brother"—headed west to Tarshish (the end of the known world, 2000 miles away, on the opposite end of the Mediterranean) rather than east to Nineveh. To get away from the presence of the Lord and the repugnance of the lost, he set sail from Joppa. His cruise would be interrupted, to say the least, but Joppa would be a reminder of graceless prejudice for centuries.

In the New Testament, Joppa was the place of Gentile inclusion. Thankfully, Joppa would make another appearance in the Bible's salvation history. In Acts 10—nearly 800 years later—we learn what Paul Harvey would call "the rest of the story." Once again the Lord has to deal with a less-than-eager messenger. This time it's Peter. Once again the question at hand is the preaching of God's message to a Gentile audience. And once again the focal point of the discussion is the little town of Joppa. The word "Joppa" occurs so many times in the text that it's obvious that it holds a symbolic significance (Acts 9:36, 38, 42, 43; 10:5, 8, 23, 32; 11:5, 13). In a wonderful display of ironic sovereignty, the Lord made Joppa the place from which the message of the Gospel would emphatically launch to the Gentiles, once and for all. Despite Peter's protestations, God used the thrice-repeated visions of the "sheet of meat" to teach a lesson that is infinitely more important than dietary laws: God, who has no prejudice (Acts 10:34; 11:12), makes unclean things clean (Acts 10:15)—including not just cuts of meat, but classes of men (Acts 11:18).

The book of Jonah vividly displays the hard-heartedness of those who have received God's undeserved grace but refuse to extend it to others. The lack of concern of Jonah for the lost—the utter hatred!—is shocking. However, it is no less shocking when we who have been so lavishly forgiven ignore the needs of fellow "Ninevites" around the world. We, like Jonah, are quick to rejoice that "salvation is of the Lord" when we consider our own deliverance (Jonah 2:9). And we, like Jonah, are reluctant to share that same message of saving grace outside our own borders (Jonah 1, 4). Whether we resent unbelievers as Jonah did or simply neglect them, the result is the same—their damnation. Let Joppa serve as a memorial of man's selfishness and God's sovereign grace. And take part in launching the Gospel around the globe.

Let the Gospel which delivered you inspire you to evangelize fellow sinners. —CHRIS

"AND THEY RETURNED HOME"

Kneeling down on the beach, we prayed and said farewell to one another.
Then we went on board the ship, and they returned home. ACTS 21:5-6

When you read the book of Acts, with whom do you identify? Many of us try to identify with a central character like Paul. Naturally so. When we read about Paul's courageous journeys and life-threatening predicaments, we tend to put ourselves in the shoes of the hero. But, as you've surely learned from experience, this approach to reading Acts is immensely discouraging! When we compare ourselves with Paul, we come up short in every respect. We end up saying to ourselves, "I'll never be as zealous, as bold, as fruitful, or as significant as Paul."

As exemplary as Paul's heart and life are for us (see Day 19), God doesn't call most of us to travel like he traveled or to accomplish what he accomplished. Next time you read through the book of Acts, look for the "normal" people—the majority of Christians. You'll quickly realize that relatively few believers planted churches, trained pastors, and were imprisoned for the Gospel. Most of the Christians (like those in Acts 20 and 21) are unnamed believers who loved and prayed for Paul, but rarely met him. For those of us who aren't called to be missionaries, but are instead called to "return home" after sending them on their way, I suggest the following lessons.

Most Christians aren't missionaries; we're missionary evidence. Missionaries *plant* churches. Most Christians *are* churches. Like the elders at Ephesus (20:36-38), the Christian families at Tyre (21:3-6), and "the brothers" in Ptolemais (21:7), most Christians are called to day-in-day-out life in local churches. We're the evidence that the Gospel once planted in our community has taken root and is continuing to grow. In reading the book of Acts, most of us shouldn't ask, "How many oceans have I sailed for the Gospel's sake?" but rather, "If Paul made a seven-day stop in my town, would he be likely to find me faithfully advancing the Gospel with the rest of the disciples in my church?"

Most Christians aren't missionaries; we're missionary admirers. It appears that Paul was a hero in the eyes of most Christians throughout Acts (including its author, Luke). When believers heard he was in town, they flocked to be with him. Most Christians considered it their privilege to hear his missionary updates and see him off. When we read Acts, rather than asking, "Have I done as many heroic things as Paul?" most of us should ask ourselves, "Do I have a deep admiration for our church's missionaries? When one of our missionaries drops by on furlough, do I make it a priority to be with him? Do I esteem missionaries as highly as their great work deserves?"

Most Christians aren't missionaries; we're missionary supporters. Notice how the Christians at Ephesus, Tyre, Ptolemais, Caesarea, and Jerusalem were united in heart with Paul. They greeted him when he arrived, housed him, spent time with him, prayed with him, kissed him goodbye, and cried at his departure. Their support was intensely personal and emotional. What an example for those of us who are called to "return home!" When reading Acts, don't ask, "How many times have I said farewell to loved ones for the Gospel?" but, "Can I really say that my heart is entwined with the burdens, joys, and concerns of the missionaries that my church supports? Do I know them? Do I pray for them? Do I communicate with them? Have I done anything that would convince them of my care for them?"

The Lord calls most of us to "return home." Back home He calls us to be faithful church members that deeply admire and wholeheartedly support missionaries.

Let the Gospel's advance on the frontlines drive your oh-so-normal life at home. —JOE

LAMBS AMONG WOLVES

Go your ways: behold, I send you forth as lambs among wolves. LUKE 10:3

A few years ago I traveled to the Pakistani town of Sangla Hill shortly after the Christian community there was attacked by a Muslim mob. After spending a day with my hurting brothers and sisters, I wrote:

> A full moon rises over the canefields around Sangla Hill, and in the twilight a minaret looks like a stake driven through the heart of this city. Three hundred Christian families live here, and not one of them feels safe tonight. My mind is swirling with all I've seen today—charred crosses, churches and homes gutted by fire, the cries of children, and the pleas of their parents for someone to protect them. The only comfort any of us have found today has been from the Scripture. Standing outside the charred remains of the Salvation Army Church, a believer named Gulzar came up to me to talk. His broken English was mended by a winning smile and joyful countenance. Gulzar told me that two promises helped him face the fear—and then he began to quote from John 14, *"Let not your heart be troubled … In my Father's house are many mansions … I go to prepare a place for you. And if I go and prepare a place for you, I will come again and receive you unto myself: that where I am, there ye may be also."* And then my dear brother lifted my spirits and gave meaning to all I have witnessed today. *"Be faithful unto death,"* Gulzar said, quoting our Lord, *"and I will give thee a crown of life."*

The next day I looked into the face of persecution again. A pastor named Masih was lying outside the hospital on a concrete walkway. The pastor had protested to the police in his village after drunken Muslims had assaulted some women in his church. For that, a Muslim gang attacked him, kicking in his skull, severing his ear, and leaving him blind in one eye. The hospital had bandaged over his wounds and thrown him out. It seems that animals get better treatment than Christians there.

Persecution and opposition have always accompanied the advance of the Gospel, but we miss something very important if we look at persecution as simply "bad things happening to good people." Persecution is tied to the very nature of the Gospel and is essential to its progress. Our persecution is linked to Christ's own sufferings (Philippians 3:7-10, Colossians 1:24; 1 Peter 4:12,13). Our persecution has many divine purposes, even if they don't make sense to us (Genesis 50:15-21; Acts 7:54-60; Acts 9:10-15). And our persecution glorifies God. His Word advances as His people demonstrate trust, hope, love, and grace while suffering for Him (2 Corinthians 6:3-10; Philippians 1:12-14; Hebrews 10:32-36; 1 Peter 4:14-16).

For Christians in many lands, life is caught somewhere between faith and fear. It brings to mind one of the Gospel's great missionary passages. The Lord Jesus told His followers that He was sending them out as "lambs among wolves" (Luke 10:3). How could He do such a thing—sending His people unarmed into the jaws of death? He could because He did so Himself. From Gethsemane to Golgotha, the Lamb not only walked among wolves, but even "gave Himself a ransom for all" (1 Timothy 2:6). And as Christ explained in Matthew 10:24-25, "A disciple is not above his teacher, nor a servant above his master. It is enough for the disciple to be like his teacher, and the servant like his master." Christians who live among wolves bring Light to dark places by their lives—and sometimes by their deaths. And they find comfort in His company.

Let the Gospel be evident in your response to persecution. —TIM

FROM GOD, THROUGH GOD & TO GOD

The gospel of God, which he promised beforehand through his prophets in the holy Scriptures, concerning his Son, ...to bring about the obedience of faith for the sake of his name among all the nations. ROMANS 1:1–5

So which Gospel do you preach? There's quite a choice, you know. From the earliest days, Satan attacked the church with counterfeit gospels. So Paul and the other apostles counterattacked with long swords of well-reasoned discourse (Romans, Hebrews, etc.) and daggers of pithy Gospel summary, the most famous being 1 Corinthians 15:3-8. Of all the Gospel daggers, the most complete is Romans 1:1-5, the "Creation to Christ" of Gospel summaries. And it's as beautiful as it is comprehensive. Notice the balanced, chiastic structure below, with Christ at the very center.

The Source of the Gospel: God. ("The gospel of God ...") No human could have invented the Gospel. It's God's idea from start to finish. God the Father, God the Son, and God the Holy Spirit decided from eternity past to save lost mankind by sending the Son to be our Savior. All three members of the Trinity are equal participants in the Gospel and are mentioned in this summary statement. The Gospel is something that "God promised" to us, not something that we promise to Him, as in other religions. Any gospel that doesn't originate with God is not the Gospel.

> *The Preparation of the Gospel: The Prophets.* ("... which he promised ...") Paul's opponents evidently charged him with novelty, but the good news of Jesus Christ didn't start with Paul or even with the birth of Christ. The good news was prophesied hundreds of times in the Old Testament across a span of thousands of years. The first prophecy even goes all the way back to the Garden of Eden, where God told Satan that the "seed of the woman" would crush the serpent's head (Genesis 3:15). In fact, the entire Old Testament is a preparation for the coming of the Savior. Any gospel not foretold by the prophets is not the Gospel.

> > *The Heart of the Gospel: The Lord Jesus Christ.* ("... concerning his Son ...") At the very core of God's redemptive plan is the incarnation, death, resurrection, and exaltation of the Son of God. Paul gives Him four exalted titles in these verses: The Son of God! The Son of God in Power! Christ! Lord! Jesus is the genius of the Gospel! Any gospel without Christ at the center is not the Gospel.

> *The Messengers of the Gospel: The Apostles.* ("... we have received grace and apostleship ...") Just as God sent the Old Testament prophets to prepare the way for Messiah, He also appointed the New Testament apostles to be witnesses of Christ and to proclaim His good news to the world. We have in the Scriptures a foundation laid by both the prophets and apostles (Ephesians 2:20). Any gospel that changes the message of the apostles is not the Gospel.

The Recipients of the Gospel: All the Nations. ("... among all the nations.") Just as the Gospel has a source (God Himself), it also has a target ("all the nations"). It's not good news for just one nation or race, but for all. Any gospel that doesn't save people from all nations is not the Gospel.

But what's the point? Why did God go through all this hassle, spend all this time, and spend the life of His only begotten Son? *"For the sake of his name"* (v. 5). Plaster that on every banner in your church; make it the theme of your life and your message to the world. The goal of the Gospel of Jesus Christ is to make God famous in every tribe and tongue and language and people. Since He isn't yet, we still have missions.

Let the Gospel's goal of magnifying God's fame in every corner of God's world be the passion of your life. —JD

BRETHREN, PRAY FOR US
That the word of the Lord may have free course. 2 THESSALONIANS 3:1

I'm not trying to be a killjoy, but one of my least favorite children's songs is "Be a Missionary Every Day." First, not all Christians are meant to be missionaries. What's more, it teaches kids that the missionary task is "up to you." Where's the Spirit there? Or the local church? Scripture, anyone? Okay, I concede that it's a helpful song insofar as it urges kids to share their faith and think about going to faraway continents. But it's as awkward to me as if we composed a song called "Be a Pastor Every Day."

We have so lowered our standards for what normal Christianity is supposed to look like that we have come to think that anything altruistic or evangelistic is missions. Loving orphans, feeding bellies, healing bodies, and saving souls are expected of every believer (Matthew 5:16, Acts 8:4). But missions is something more specific. It is "the sending forth of authorized persons beyond the borders of the New Testament church and her immediate Gospel influence to proclaim the Gospel of Jesus Christ in Gospel-destitute areas …" (George Peters, *A Biblical Theology of Missions*, p. 11).

But don't get the idea that you're exempt from missions because you're not a missionary. The front lines require supply lines. Both demand equal sacrifice; neither is more valuable than the other (1 Corinthians 12:14-15). It's not complicated: if you're not sent, you send. You send by *paying* and *praying* for the mission.

When I first knew God wanted me to be a missionary, I loathed the idea of raising support. Didn't want to be a "moochinary." Another missionary rebuked me and said, "That's just pride." Pride?! I was thinking it was humility! "False humility," he said. "Self-sufficiency. Don't you get it? You're giving people the chance to climb Albanian mountains with you!" *Wow,* I thought, *that was either a clever spin or a brilliant truth.* As it turns out, he was right on. Paul was supported financially by the Philippian church, and he told them that he didn't want their money as much as he wanted spiritual fruit to abound to *their* account (Philippians 4:15-17). When I report to a supporting church, I don't talk about "my" ministry; I talk about "our" ministry. Missions is an eternal investment partnership. How's your portfolio doing?

Missionaries mean it when they tell you, "What we *really* need is your prayers!" We can do without money (Paul sometimes made tents), but we can't do without prayers. The "Gospel-destitute areas" see us as criminal combatants, not friends (Colossians 4:2-4). We're up against reigning principalities, religious powers, radical politicians, and recurring persecution. We get attacked from the front, from the rear, from the sides, and, yes, even from within (2 Corinthians 7:5). Missionaries aren't special. There is nothing about our foreign geography that makes us super-sanctified or sin-proof. We're tempted to deny like Peter, pout like Elijah, get cynical like Jonah, and turn back like John Mark. We deal with depression and loneliness and pain and threats and fears and danger and frustration. Our women and children get injured in the fray. Our new converts get attacked worse than we do. War is hell. So *please*, pray! When you do, sure, pray for our safety (Romans 15:30-31; 2 Thessalonians 3:2), but please don't exert all your time there. Jesus made it clear that mission work is exceedingly unsafe, so we're already past that hump. We'd love to avoid pain, but not at the expense of boldness; Christ must be lifted up at any cost (Philippians 1:20-21). So pore over our prayer letters (and reply once in a while). And when you pray, pray the prayer that Paul requested: *that the word of the Lord would spread quickly and be glorified* (2 Thessalonians 3:1). That's the crux of the matter. That's the reason we came.

Let the Gospel drive you to your knees (as in, right now). —DAVID

Solomon's Temple & Missions

When a foreigner, who is not of your people Israel, comes from a far country for your name's sake (for they shall hear of your great name and your mighty hand, and of your outstretched arm).... 1 KINGS 8:41–42

There are several contrasts between the Old and New Testaments, but God's heart for the nations is not one of them! From Abraham's call (Genesis 12:3) to Israel's exodus (Exodus 14:18) to David's battle with Goliath (1 Samuel 17:46) to Solomon's magnificent temple (1 Kings 8:60), God has always been concerned that His glory be recognized by people from every nation. Solomon's prayer at the temple's dedication reveals that God had at least two missionary purposes for the temple in Jerusalem. Each of them directly applies to the missionary mindset of the New Testament church, which is the temple of the living God (1 Corinthians 3:17; Ephesians 2:19-22; 1 Peter 2:5).

The temple was a place of praise. Solomon was certain that foreigners would come to the temple as they heard how God had saved His people (1 Kings 8:41-42). With a "mighty hand" and "outstretched arm" God had brought Israel out of Egypt—Think the ten plagues, the pillar of fire, the Red Sea's opening and closing, and the daily provision in the wilderness for forty years (Deuteronomy 4:34; 5:15; 7:19; 11:2-3; 26:8; Psalm 136:10-18). News of these mighty acts spread quickly (as Rahab explained in Joshua 2:10-11). For centuries, God's reputation had grown among the nations. Now, Solomon's temple was where they could come to learn more about Him. The temple was the center of worship, where the people whom God had powerfully delivered would praise Him for His mighty salvation. Similarly, the church, God's new temple, is both the evidence of God's saving power and the echo of it. We have experienced personal salvation from sin through faith in Christ, and we regularly come together to "proclaim the excellencies of Him who called [us] out of darkness into His marvelous light" (1 Peter 2:9). And as Solomon said of the old temple, the result of unbelievers observing our worship should be the growth of God's fame (1 Corinthians 14:25). When lost people enter your church, do they see the evidence of God's saving power in His people? Do they hear you praising God for the wondrous things He's done in Christ?

The temple was a place of prayer. The temple was "a house of prayer for all the nations" (Mark 11:7; Isaiah 56:7). Solomon was certain that foreigners would come to the temple and pray, that the Lord would answer, and that God's fame would spread all the more (I Kings 8:43). People would pray for forgiveness or victory or restoration, and God would answer (8:30-50). As at Solomon's temple of old, God's church should be devoted to prayer (Acts 2:42), even more so now that we have direct access through Christ (Hebrews 4:14-16; 10:19-22). In particular, we should pray as Solomon did for God's glory to be revealed to people "from a far country" (8:41). Our prayers should be evangelistic in both content and intent. We should pray specifically for the Gospel's advance among the lost. And we should pray so that when God answers, the lost are convinced that He is great and we are His people.

God used the Old Testament temple to show His glory to the nations as they came to Jerusalem. Likewise, God desires that we, the church—His New Testament temple—spread His fame among the nations, both as they are attracted to us and as we go to them. God's glory will spread as we exalt His saving power and experience His answers to our prayers.

Let the Gospel's advance inflame your corporate praise and prayer. —JOE

Pentecost & Missions

Tongues as of fire...rested on each one of them. ACTS 2:3

In 2010 I was privileged to be near Jerusalem on the day of Pentecost. It was a rush to contemplate that the world-changing events of Acts 2 occurred just miles from where I stood. Pentecost was a day bursting with historical significance—the "birthday" of the New Testament church. It was also a day filled with tremendous *missionary* significance. The church born on Pentecost was unmistakably a *missionary church*. The church was made for missions, as Acts 2 demonstrates in three ways.

Pentecost signified the mobility of the missionary church. For ten days following Jesus' ascension, His followers waited in Jerusalem, as ordered (Acts 1:4-5). "Suddenly," on Pentecost morning, the Holy Spirit came upon them in a new and powerful way (2:2). His arrival was announced by three signs: a rushing wind (2:2), flames of fire that hovered over each of their heads (2:3), and the ability to speak in unknown languages (2:4). The last of these gets the most press, but the first two are stunning. They take us back to two Old Testament parallels—other times when God "moved in" to a new home. When Moses dedicated the tabernacle, Jehovah showed His presence by filling the tabernacle with His glory and hovering over it as a cloudy or fiery pillar (Exodus 40:34-38). Similarly, when Solomon dedicated the temple, God's "housewarming" was demonstrated by an overwhelming cloud and by fire descending from heaven as God's glory filled the temple (2 Chronicles 5:13-14; 7:1-3). Those same signs—most notably the hovering flames—were now present at Pentecost, powerfully portraying God's residence in a new temple: the church of Jesus Christ, and the individuals who comprise it! God's mediating presence on earth was no longer a stationary tent or building, but a *people* (1 Corinthians 3:16-17; Ephesians 2:21; 1 Peter 2:5). Worship was no longer tied to Jerusalem, or to any single location (John 4:20-24). God's temple had been *franchised* and *mobilized*, prepared for the Great Commission. Rather than inviting the nations to "Come!" to Jerusalem, the new temple—the church!—was commanded and enabled to "Go!" to the nations.

Pentecost signified the harvest of the missionary church. The feast of Pentecost was a celebration of God's blessing His people with bountiful harvest (Leviticus 23:15-22; Numbers 28:26-31). Inaugurating His church on that particular day was powerfully symbolic. What better way to foretell the gathering of souls that would come about through the church's ministry than to use a festival celebrating harvest? There would indeed be a harvest in the newly established church, but it would be *spiritual*—a Gospel ingathering (John 4:35; Matthew 9:36-38; 1 Corinthians 3:5-9). The reaping of souls began on day one, with over 3000 coming to Christ and being baptized (2:41).

Pentecost signified the multi-ethnicity of the missionary church. The international and multi-cultural nature of the church is unmistakably foreshadowed in Acts 2. The disciples were granted the ability to speak in unlearned languages (2:4-11). It wasn't nonsensical babble, nor was it merely a miracle of hearing. They spoke diverse languages. Why? Certainly tongues was a sign (1 Corinthians 14:22). But why *that* sign? Why not a flashing light or an announcement from heaven? Because the use of multiple languages signified in a powerful, vivid way the missionary nature of God's new program. This concept is advanced further when Scripture catalogues for us the various nationalities that were present in Jerusalem that first Christian Pentecost—from regions north, south, east, and west of Jerusalem (2:9-11). Christianity wasn't a Jewish thing, or a Hebrew thing, or a Greek thing. It wasn't culturally monolithic. The Gospel would work all over the world, in various cultures and in various tongues. Indeed, it *has*.

Let the Gospel mobilize you to reap a universal harvest. —CHRIS

He Showed Them His Hands

When he had said this, he showed them his hands and his side. Then the disciples were glad when they saw the Lord. Jesus said to them again, "Peace be with you. As the Father has sent me, even so I am sending you."

JOHN 20:20-21

The cross has always been central to the Great Commission—both its message and its method. John 20:20-21 records the first giving of the Great Commission after the resurrection. The connection between Christ's sacrifice and the sending of His disciples could not have been clearer. As He showed them the marks of the wounds in His hands, He pointed out that in the same way the Father sent Him—that is, the way of the cross—"even so I am sending you." It is interesting that the disciples recognized Him by His scars. Although His body was perfect and glorified, the marks of Calvary remained. This is a gracious thing He has done, for one day we, too, shall recognize our Savior by these marks of grace and sacrifice.

As the disciples went out to reach their world, the cross was always in view. The Lord had been preparing them for this. In Matthew 16:24-25, Jesus told the disciples, "If anyone would come after me, let him deny himself and take up his cross and follow me. For whoever would save his life will lose it, but whoever loses his life for my sake will find it." There are three things in view here.

Cross-bearing. ("Take up his cross.") What did Jesus mean that a disciple must "take up his cross"? What did it mean to those who first heard it? For us, the cross is a symbol of love, but in the first century, the cross was definitely not a symbol of love—it was a symbol of hate. For us the cross is a symbol of life, but in Jesus' day it was plainly a symbol of death and shame. The Lord had just told His disciples that He *must* go to Jerusalem and suffer and take up the cross (Matthew 16:21). So cross-bearing is fully embracing, fully following, fully identifying with Jesus—whatever that will mean for you and wherever He will lead you.

Risk-taking. ("Whoever loses his life for my sake will find it.") Risk-taking should be a lifestyle for the Christian. However it doesn't involve foolishness; it involves a proper view of life and of our Lord. It means not letting fear dominate our decisions. It means believing Matthew 16:25—you can't save your life, you can only spend it. Spending life well means investing it for maximum impact for Christ! When I was growing up, my mother kept a plaque on the wall above the kitchen sink. After all these years, the old lines are not trite but focused like a laser on what matters:

> *"Only one life, 'twill soon be past.*
> *Only what's done for Christ will last."*

Fellowship. ("Follow me.") Following Christ is about wanting to be as near to Him as possible. Graciously, He has also promised to be near us. In another giving of the Great Commission, the passage in Matthew 28:18-20, Jesus gave His disciples their final, impossible orders: "Go therefore and make disciples of all nations." It was a task far beyond their ability—but not beyond His, for the King with scars in His hands said, "All authority in heaven and on earth has been given to me … And behold, I am with you always." When Jesus sent His disciples out to evangelize a hostile world, He did not say it would be easy. He only promised His presence—and that is enough.

Let the Gospel remind you of the cross—His and yours. —TIM

Two Great Omissions

Go therefore and make disciples of all nations, baptizing them in the name of the Father and of the Son and of the Holy Spirit, teaching them to observe all that I have commanded you. MATTHEW 28:19-20

It would be disastrous if we messed up our marching orders from Jesus. But how could we go wrong when the orders are so simple? The Great Commission is really just one main command to "make disciples," followed by two descriptions of how that's to be done. The phrase "baptizing them" reminds us that the short-term component, which began with preaching the Gospel, must culminate in people putting their faith in Christ and being baptized into the Triune Name. Then comes the longer-term component, teaching the baptized disciple to obey all of Christ's commands—a task which lasts a lifetime. Simple enough. Yet, in every age, Satan has tried to derail both the short-term and long-term components. Here are two ways he's doing it these days.

Disciple Nations? It's becoming wildly popular in modern Christianity to read "make disciples of all nations" as a command to "disciple nations." (There's even a book called *Discipling Nations.*) In this view, it's not enough to evangelize individuals; mission work must attempt to change the very structures of civil and governmental society to be more in line with God's standards of justice and righteousness. The problem is, you can't get this idea from the Great Commission. "Nations" here refers to ethnic entities, not nation-states with their laws and governments. "Disciples" always refers to people—apprentices who attach themselves to a teacher. How does a nation-state become a disciple? And how exactly does one go about baptizing a nation?

Missions as "changing the structures of society" always leads to a muting of the Gospel. I've noticed that most "holistic" mission agencies do little or no evangelism. (Ironically, the old-style missionaries, reproached by the "holistic-er than thou" groups, spend much of their time helping with physical and social needs. Which group ends up being more holistic?) There's no doubt that the church has to get better at contending for justice and defending the cause of the alien, the fatherless, and the widow. The Gospel makes us care desperately about alleviating human suffering. But missions that seeks to alleviate suffering in this life without seeking even more desperately to alleviate suffering in the life to come is not missions that is faithful to the Great Commission.

Everything Christ commanded? Okay, so most of us aren't going to fall for the latest Social Gospel fad. Good. But how are we doing with the next part of the Great Commission: "teaching them to observe all that I have commanded you"? Not very well, it seems to me. The command isn't all that complicated. It requires that we read Matthew, Mark, Luke, and John with our baptized disciples (not neglecting the rest of the New Testament, which is really "The Gospels Unpacked"), and then help them obey all the commands by the power of the Holy Spirit. We're not talking about a million commands or even a thousand. I doubt that you could come up with a hundred.

Yet, as simple as the directive is, how many of us are *systematically* helping Christ's apprentices obey His commands? Conservative Christianity has tended in the last 150 years to deemphasize the Gospels. (Maybe it's a reaction to the hijacking of the Gospels by liberals a hundred years ago, or the influence of early dispensationalism that taught that passages like the Sermon on the Mount were not intended mainly for the church.)

Satan doesn't mind which of these two errors we make. They're both disastrous. The "discipling nations" error emphasizes Christ's example at the expense of Christ's Gospel. The "ignoring Christ's commands" error emphasizes Christ's Gospel at the expense of Christ's example. Neither fulfills the Great Commission of our Great Savior.

Let the Gospel change hearts and families and cities and nations—in that order. —JD

THE EVANGELIST'S HEARTBEAT

[God has given me grace] to be a minister of Christ Jesus to the Gentiles in the priestly service of the gospel of God, so that the offering of the Gentiles may be acceptable. ROMANS 15:16

Paul invested almost twenty years of the prime of his adult life in planting about thirty strategic churches across a 1500-mile region of the Roman Empire. At times he endured sleeplessness, hunger, robbery, and shipwrecks for the sake of the Gospel. At other times he was imprisoned, stoned, and threatened with death for the message he spoke. Paul was *the* apostle to the Gentiles (Romans 11:13), and, as *the* apostle to the uncircumcised (Galatians 2:7), he will never be duplicated. Yet he was also *the* exemplary Christian (1 Corinthians 4:16; 11:1; Philippians 3:17; 4:9; 2 Timothy 1:13). Under the inspiration of God's Holy Spirit, Paul wrote, "Imitate me." So, even though we'll never imitate his remarkable giftedness or success, God calls every Christian to imitate Paul's heartbeat for getting the Gospel to those who need it. Paul had four driving motivations for proclaiming the Gospel that we should imitate.

"I want God's name to be known." The Lord had called Paul to carry His name before the Gentiles and to suffer much for the sake of His name (Acts 9:15-16; Romans 1:5). Thus, Paul's great passion was that *Christ* be "proclaimed" and that *Christ* be "honored in [his] body, whether by life or death" (Philippians 1:18-20). If you had asked Paul, "Why are you evangelizing?" he would reply, "Because I want the name of Jesus to be magnified in all nations." Is God's name your heartbeat? Does it bother you that the non-Christians around you are not magnifying Christ's name? If not, ask the Lord to give you a fresh glimpse of His unrivaled majesty today.

"I am under obligation to speak." Paul was "under obligation" to communicate the Gospel to non-Christians (Romans 1:14; 1 Corinthians 9:16-17; 2 Corinthians 5:18-19; Galatians 2:7; 2 Timothy 1:11; Ephesians 3:7-8). Similarly, every Christian is required by God to be a witness, a light, and a disciple-maker. Hudson Taylor used to say, "The Great Commission is not an option to be considered but a command to be obeyed." Do you speak the Gospel to others in joyful obedience to God's straightforward commands? If not, start obeying today.

"I want people to be saved." Paul wanted those without Christ to be rescued from their perilous condition. He fervently prayed for their salvation (Romans 10:1), lived without certain freedoms in order to see them saved (1 Corinthians 9:19-22; 1 Corinthians 10:31-11:1), and endured much persecution so that they'd be saved (2 Timothy 2:10). How much do you pray for the lost to be rescued? How many liberties have you sacrificed for their deliverance? How much discomfort have you endured for others' salvation? Christian, the lost world pursues comfort. You should *sacrifice* your comfort in pursuit of the lost world.

"I want to present an offering to Christ." In both his evangelism and discipleship, Paul always had "the Day" in view—the day when he would stand before the Lord Jesus (1 Corinthians 3:12-14; Philippians 2:15-17; Colossians 1:28-29; 1 Thessalonians 2:17-20). According to Romans 15:16, Paul lived his whole life looking toward the day when he would see Jesus and present Him an offering of people: "Here, Lord, is my life's work that I offer to You in worship. I gave my life for these people so that they would praise Your grace for all eternity." Are you motivated to evangelize, knowing that you'll soon see Jesus and offer Him your life's work? I urge you to invest in someone today in preparation for the worship you'll offer to Jesus on that day.

Let the Gospel's advance be your heartbeat. —JOE

For the Sake of His Name

Men who have risked their lives for the name of our Lord Jesus Christ.
ACTS 15:26

"Why in the world do they do it?" I've often wondered what would motivate missionaries to transplant their families to dangerous and depressing places in order to establish a Gospel beachhead. I marvel at their missionary moxie. They're my heroes. Why do they do it? *Doxology.* In plain English, *doxological ministry* means that our primary goal in evangelism is the glory of God. To quote Acts 15:26, Romans 1:5, and 3 John 7, missionaries do what they do "for the sake of Christ's name."

Missionaries take personal risks for the glory of God. Missionaries don't play it safe. They serve on the world's front lines—sometimes literally, as well as spiritually. Like Paul and Barnabas in Acts 15:26, missionaries "have risked their lives for the name of our Lord Jesus Christ." What does that look like? For Paul and Barnabas, it meant facing opposition, imprisonment, and near-martyrdom (Acts 13-14). For a man like my brother Dan, it means persevering in Brazilian church planting despite repeated break-ins, violence that once left him splattered with a neighbor's brain matter, and persecution that left a missionary friend crippled. What would motivate such audacious risk? *A longing for the glory of Christ's name.* It tethers them to the field through suffering. It fortifies them amidst despair. It is the grand cause of their lives.

Missionaries take financial risks for the glory of God. Every missionary I have ever known has been financially dependent on charitable giving. And almost every one has lived like a pauper. Like those mentioned in 3 John 7, missionaries have cast themselves on the Lord's people "for the sake of the name." I've seen this kind of gospel gutsiness in my family, as well. My brother Jeff has put his neck out for hundreds of thousands of dollars to train African believers in expository preaching and to outfit them with resources that will help them in that great endeavor. My father, Chuck, has invested a lifetime and a fortune planting several churches and publishing hundreds of thousands of pieces of Gospel literature which he distributes throughout the world. Why risk so much? Why spend so much? *A longing for the glory of Christ's name.*

The people of God should support missionaries generously for the glory of God. While the dauntless, advance-at-any-cost spirit of missionaries is heroic, the church at home must do a better job of alleviating their burdens. That's the overall point of 3 John. Verse 5 urges us to be "faithful" in supporting missionaries. Verse 6 commands us to support them "in a manner worthy of God," showing our love for Him by giving generously to His ambassadors. Verse 7 insists that Gospel work be funded by believers. And verse 8 promises that those who support missionaries are reckoned "fellow workers for the truth." (This "credit-by-association" principle mirrors the "guilt-by-association" principle of 2 John 7-11.) In light of these truths, it's clear that our missions support system needs reform. We pray for laborers, then watch those who respond to the call spend three to four years raising support. Churches often support too many missionaries for too little. Perhaps it would be better to invest more money, care, and prayer into fewer missionaries whom we support well and know well. Whatever system we utilize, there obviously is a need for more generous investment in eternity through giving to missions. We need to be as radically generous as those we're sending.

If it sounds like I'm trying to shame you into missions, I'm not. We need to be *inspired* into missions. We get to be part of a cosmic cause—the turning of rebels into worshipers who will one day bow with us around Jesus' throne (Ephesians 1:6, 12, 14; 3:20-21). We go and give *for Christ's name.*

Let the Gospel make you live and give with reckless abandon for Christ's name. —CHRIS

DARIUS & THE LIONS' DEN

Then king Darius wrote unto all people, nations, and languages.

DANIEL 6:25

Missions is the privilege of distributing the most magnificent message ever dispatched. The more I learn about the theology of other religions, the more I revel in the miracle of the cross (Galatians 6:14). Our message is infinitely superior to any other. Go ahead. Engage devout people of other faiths, and ask them for simple explanations on issues like sin, justice, mercy, forgiveness, and eternal life. You will discover that their theology has gaping holes and unresolved conflicts. Half the time, after fumbling around for an answer, they end up asking, "Well what do *you* believe about that?" (Hint, hint.)

Take Islam for example. One of its heralded "99 names of God" is *Al-'Adl*, "The Utterly Just." Another is *Ar-Rahīm*, "The Exceedingly Merciful." I often ask my Muslim friends how God can be both at the same time. By nature, justice and mercy are mutually exclusive. You don't have to be a scholar to understand the logical problem there.

Consider Daniel 6. The Median king Darius is tricked into signing a law banning prayer. Daniel will soon be caught in the act, then sentenced to the den of fangs. Darius is livid at his unscrupulous cabinet members. And he's the *king*! If I were Darius, I might have said, "Punks. Peons. You think you can play me like a pawn? Guess what, you repugnant mass of carnivore fodder? That law I just signed? Never happened." Certainly there were loophole lawyers back then too, no? But even though Darius "labored till the going down of the sun" to deliver Daniel, he couldn't (Daniel 6:14-15).

Darius understood a judicial principle that "the great religions of the world" do not: law trumps mercy. (Imagine if the primary consideration in courts of law were compassion for *criminals!*) Though Darius felt compassion for Daniel and realized how deceptively the new law had been contrived, he was still bound to enforce it. For all his authority, he couldn't concoct a merciful solution that simultaneously maintained the dignity of the law. In the end, his only recourse was to appeal to the miraculous mercy of Daniel's God (v. 16). And God delivered. The law was upheld *and* Daniel was spared (v. 22).

Browse the web of religious ideas for an answer to the problem of sin. Like Darius, you will labor in vain. There's no solution out there...that is, except the Gospel of Jesus Christ. Sinners deserve wrath but receive miraculous mercy. How? God *justifies* them. What? Pronounces them *righteous*. Huh? How is that right? Does God just make a sinner's offenses go "poof"? Absolutely not. That would undermine justice. It requires a miracle to make justice and mercy merge, and God accomplished just that at the cross. He heaped His wrath onto His holy Son and slew Him. *It's flabbergasting!* Read Paul on this in Romans 3:23-28. In merciful justice and just mercy, Jesus was thrown to the lions. They ravished Him instead of us. Thus Jesus defanged the law (Galatians 3:13, Colossians 2:14) and clothed us in the chain mail of His righteousness (Romans 8:1-3, 2 Corinthians 5:21). Now, we're eternally alive. We deserved ultimate justice, needed miraculous mercy, and got both at the cross! That's the message. And it is brilliant.

Here's where Darius' story gets radical. In the space of a few days, he went from saying, "I am God" (Daniel 6:7-9), to "God is God" (6:25-27). God's wisdom and power made him "exceedingly glad" (6:23). Then he did what *Christians* are supposed to do: he proclaimed the fame of the only true God to "all people, nations, and languages" (6:25). He didn't need a Great Commission. His proclamation was just a knee-jerk reaction, a supernaturally natural response to having met the Lord (cf. John 1:43-46, 4:28-29). Perhaps Darius was a tad overzealous, making faith in God an imperial *decree*, but the point is this: he was doing everything in his power to spread the news. Are you?

Let the Gospel's supremacy compel you to do everything in your power to spread it. —DAVID

THE GREAT CONTROVERSY

There is no other name ... by which we must be saved. ACTS 4:12

The greatest controversy in our world today isn't political or economic. It's not about Bible translations or worship style. All of those issues have their place—and adequate share of controversy—but the *great* controversy in the world is that "there is no other name under heaven given among men by which we must be saved" (Acts 4:12). There are people in the world on this day who will be thrown out of their homes or face prison or even death because they believe this. And closer to home, just try telling someone on the street or at the mall that Jesus is the only way of salvation. It will quickly be evident that the controversy isn't just on the other side of the world.

Peter's declaration to the Sanhedrin in Acts 4 is packed with life-and-death truth:

- *"Under heaven"* – across the entire world
- *"Among men"* – all people, from all nations
- *"Name"* – a specific Person, and a specific truth about that Person

The Gospel Peter preached has always been controversial. Paul wrote in 1 Corinthians 1:18, "For the word of the cross is folly to those who are perishing, but to us who are being saved, it is the power of God." He went on to point out that the deeply religious Jews and the culturally sophisticated Greeks all scoffed at this truth, and so it is in our day. What we call *Good News* others call arrogant, ridiculous, or even hate speech.

Despite these responses, the Word of the cross remains at once the *only* message and the *best* message we have to give the lost world. It is the Word that can set captives free, give sight to the blind, and raise the spiritually dead—because it is the only message that is the power of God unto salvation (Romans 1:16). But the message needs messengers—it's how the Maker of the message has designed it. "How then will they call on him in whom they have not believed? And how are they to believe in him of whom they have never heard? And how are they to hear without someone preaching" (Romans 10:14)? Near the end of his extraordinary ministry, Samuel Zwemer ("The Apostle to Islam") preached the following:

> It is time that a protest be made against the misuse of the word "evangelism." It has only one etymological, New Testament, historical, and theological connotation; namely, to tell the good news of One who came to earth to die on the cross for us: who rose again and who ever lives to intercede with those who repent and believe the Gospel. To evangelize is to win disciples, to become fishers of men, to carry the Gospel message directly to all the nations .... If we are ashamed of the Gospel message our lives will not be radiant. ("The Cross and the Great Commission")

Radiant. There must have been something of that about Peter and John, for who were these men to speak such things to the supreme court of the land? They were without credentials or degrees. Educated or not, they preached the Gospel, as unpopular as it was. There was something about Peter and John, something about their courage, something about the stand-alone force of their words, something ... no, *Someone.* I'm sure the faces of Caiaphas and his cronies turned pale—"Didn't we get rid of Him? Crucified—buried—gone for good?" The Person who wouldn't go away was now reflected in the faces and words of His disciples, and there was no denying it. "They recognized that they had been with Jesus" (Acts 4:13).

The Great Controversy—*The Name-that-is-above-every-name Controversy*—is not about arguing. It's about speaking of the Savior clearly, humbly, and boldly, and doing so in a way that reminds people of Jesus.

Let the Gospel embolden you to proclaim the controversial, soul-saving truth. —TIM

CHRISTLIKE COMPASSION

When he saw the crowds, he had compassion for them. MATTHEW 9:36

Matthew 9:35-38 is a heart-stirring depiction of Christ's compassion for the harassed and shepherdless multitudes. It appears at first glance that Jesus was moved by a faceless throng, the way we might feel while watching masses of humanity as they bow toward Mecca, wind through a bazaar, or sit in numb silence in a refugee camp. We think of multitudes in a non-personal, distant way. But Jesus didn't see just a crowd. He saw individuals—real people with real needs. His pity on the multitudes and His lamenting call for laborers in Matthew 9:35-38 climax two chapters in which He repeatedly engaged sufferers and sinners face to face, providing a model of compassionate ministry for every believer. Look again at Matthew 8-9, and ask the Lord to help you see people as Jesus did.

Matthew 8:1 bridges the gap between the Sermon on the Mount and a series of miracles. Having just preached the best sermon in history, Jesus was descending the hillside amidst throngs of people (8:1). They gathered around Christ as though He were a living magnet, perhaps wanting to thank Him, or ask Him a question, or have Him sign their Bibles. (Okay, I made that last part up.) Try to imagine the exhilaration and exhaustion you would feel after delivering such a message to such an assembly. Christ, however, refused to get caught up in the enthusiasm of the moment. Instead, He used the opportunity to demonstrate how very different His recently-announced kingdom would be from the world's. Unexpectedly, in the midst of the commotion, Jesus' attention was arrested by the most unlikely of people. A leper called out to Him for mercy (8:2). Lepers were the most feared people of Jesus' day—exiled and reviled by men, tortured by a creeping, nibbling death. We might expect the Lord to pass the beggar by, perhaps muttering something to him about making an appointment. But we misunderstand our Savior. Christ shocked the multitude by stopping for the man—by listening to him, by pitying him, by *touching* him and healing him (8:3).

This is but one example of Christ's engagement of individuals. Matthew 8 and 9 go on to tell several similar stories of Christ's attentiveness and compassion. He healed a centurion's servant (8:5-13). He restored an aged mother-in-law (8:14-15). He rescued two demoniacs (8:28-34). He healed and forgave a man who was physically and spiritually paralyzed (9:1-8). He reached out to tax collectors and sinners (9:9-13). He delivered a man's daughter from death (9:18-19, 23-26). He healed a desperate woman of a hemorrhage (9:20-22). He gave sight to two blind men (9:27-31). He restored speech and sense to a demon-possessed mute (9:32-34). As if all that weren't enough, we're twice told that He ministered to countless others in the same way (8:16-17; 9:35). Christ was moved by individuals—young and old, male and female, rich and poor, Jew and Gentile, revered and reviled.

A missionary friend of mine has provoked me to this kind of Christlike compassion by urging me to "learn the story behind the face." We live in a broken world, filled with broken people. Not just mobs in markets and mosques. *Individuals.* A single mom. A successful but empty man. An athletic teenager. An addict. An abused child. A widow. An intellectual. An AIDS patient. A loving father. A prostitute.

The world is indeed a ripe harvest. Pray for laborers. And be part of the answer to that prayer by pitying broken people, just like Jesus did. Notice them. Listen to them. Engage them with the Gospel. "Learn the story behind the face," and enter into it—one person at a time.

Let the Gospel produce in you a Christlike compassion for real people. —CHRIS

GLOBAL COOLING

For I am not ashamed of the gospel of Christ: for it is the power of God unto salvation. ROMANS 1:16

The Apostle Paul, like all roads, was headed to Rome (1:15). The believers in the imperial capital were surrounded by such a muck of materialism that he would soon implore them, "Be not conformed to this world" (12:2). In a Roman world of competing gods and compelling goods, it might have been easy for a believer to be shy with the Gospel. The cross certainly isn't *posh*. But Paul crafted his masterpiece to ensure that his Roman brethren knew that the Gospel is *potent*. Power-of-God potent!

Americans often ask missionaries, "Now that materialism has crept into your corner of the globe, are people becoming colder to the Gospel?" They assume that as the world becomes more and more like one giant superstore, the numbing allure of stuff will hinder the Gospel's advance. Hogwash. Stuff is no match for "the power of God."

I am reminded of my faithful co-laborer Astrit, who serves Christ in an austere, hostile environment in the Albanian Alps. To him, the suggestion that materialism makes unbelievers cold to the Gospel sounds like an excuse to quit fishing. He gets agitated at this notion and replies, "Perhaps some Albanians are becoming cold to the Gospel— *but not the unbelieving ones! It* is the *believers* who are becoming cold. We have become materialistic. We have lost our passion to save people from the fire" (Jude 1:23).

Lost people have always been cold to the Gospel. To use the terminology of Ephesians 2, they are *dead* to the Gospel. We expect corpses to be cold, but not the living. That's why Christians get rebuked for lukewarmness, not the lost (Revelation 3:15-17). The problem with most Christians is that we have come to expect people to reject the Gospel, so we give up. We've lost our confidence in the thawing, life-giving, supernatural blaze of the Holy Spirit. Astrit's ministry is so powerful because he *expects* people to repent and believe. Yes, he knows the frustration of bleak, wintery seasons of ministry. But when his fishing waters freeze over, he doesn't give up. He simply drills a hole and goes ice fishing, knowing that the fish will bite again soon.

Evangelism-killing pessimism is nothing new. Roland Allen took aim at it in 1927 with his helpful book *Missionary Methods: St. Paul's or Ours?* He writes,

> Paul expected his hearers to be moved …. This expectation is a very real part of the presentation of the Gospel. It is a form of faith …. Simply to scatter the seed, with a sort of vague hope that some of it may come up somewhere, is not preaching the Gospel. It is indeed a misrepresentation of the Gospel. To preach the Gospel requires … that the speaker should expect a response. (p. 74)

What a challenge: "Expect a response!" We must never try to gauge the potential of a sinner's conversion. We tend to look at people and say, "This gal would make a great Christian" or "That people group will never turn to Christ." That is a Christless way to look at the lost. The first statement assumes some natural merit in the sinner. The second denies the Savior's power. And both are highly presumptuous, as if God has granted us a sudden gust of omniscience or the prerogative of choosing who gets to hear. Our job is simply to proclaim the faith, faithfully and expectantly. Yes, some will reject the Truth, and others will delay, but some will believe (Acts 17:32-34).

No Satanic effort to halt the advance of the Gospel can be ultimately successful, but perhaps the Devil's best strategy to date is this global cooling of the Church through our own materialism and defeatist attitudes. Have the people around us become cold to the Gospel? Perhaps the better question is this: *Have we?*

Let the Gospel reignite your faith in its power to save. —DAVID

ONE DAY TO LIVE

And I tell you, make friends for yourselves by means of unrighteous wealth, so that when it fails they may receive you into the eternal dwellings. LUKE 16:9

I have less than one day to live. It helps me to divide my life into just three stages, three "days," each one around 25 years long. The first got me past college and into marriage. The second began my adult life and took me to middle age. The sun's already rising on my third and final day that will take me to my dotage. How many days do you have left? If you're in college, the sun's already setting on your first day, and you have just two left. If you think the first day went by fast, you don't know what fast is.

And so the Bible piles metaphor on top of simile on top of word picture to convince you that your life is short. You're a fading flower. A mist. Grass. Dew. A shadow. Chaff. Smoke. From Job to James, God says that you will live a very, very short life followed by a very, very long eternity (Job 14:1-2; Psalm 39:4-5; 90:5-6; 103:15; James 4:14).

In light of this, I'm completely taken by Christ's story in Luke 16:1-9 about a CEO who heard that one of his managers was crooked. He called him in and fired him on the spot. Well, not quite on the spot. He gave him a little time to get his accounts in order and turned in—maybe a day, maybe two. Hmmm. Sound familiar?

What would he do with his last day? He had a plan, a shrewd plan that would impact his future. With the last bit of authority he had left, he called in everyone who owed his boss money and, to their delight, gave them huge discounts on what they owed! The boss knew he'd been beaten, but what could he do? Managers have authority to do things like that, even managers on the last day of their job. (By the way, we don't have to explain away this guy's sin; Jesus called him "dishonest" in 16:8. The point of the parable is shrewdness, not honesty.)

It sure makes it easy on the Bible student when Jesus interprets His own parable: "For the sons of this world are more shrewd in dealing with their own generation than the sons of light" (16:8). This is not a compliment to "sons of light." He's saying we Christians are often stupid—we don't live consistently with the reality that we have just one or two "days" left on this planet and eternity stretching out before us. The world often lives more consistently with its values than we do. This manager leveraged every last ounce of his rapidly-fading authority to secure great advantage for his future. He was shrewd. How about us? Jesus implies that we're more like a manager who spends his last day redecorating the office that he will soon vacate.

Christ follows up His interpretation of the parable with an application: "And I tell you, make friends for yourselves by means of unrighteous wealth, so that when it fails they may receive you into the eternal dwellings" (16:9). Unrighteous wealth? He's talking about your money and possessions. Eternal dwellings? He's talking about heaven! Who's going to receive you into heaven? All those people who became your friends, and then your brothers and sisters, because of the shrewd way you took your tiny bit of worldly wealth and your rapidly-fading time and leveraged them for eternal results.

It's all about Gospel leveraging. You and I don't have much. We're not so gifted. We don't have much money. Our time's almost gone. But that's what leveraging is all about. The Gospel has the power to compound interest for eternity, so that even a very small investment will yield unbelievable returns. The Lord Jesus is telling you to take your worldly wealth and fleeting time and put them to Gospel use. The people you impact will line the streets to greet you when you come home to heaven. Leverage your life for God's eternal glory and your eternal joy. (Continued tomorrow.)

Let the Gospel and eternity determine how you use your time and money. —JD

The Shrewd & His Money

One who is faithful in a very little is also faithful in much, and one who is dishonest in a very little is also dishonest in much. LUKE 16:10

They say a fool and his money are soon parted, but according to Scripture, the opposite is true: A fool and his money aren't parted soon enough. That's the point of Luke 16:10. You might be surprised to find out that this verse isn't really talking about how if you're faithful at small tasks, God will entrust you with larger ones. That's doubtless true, but that's not where the Lord's going with this.

The key to understanding Luke 16:10 is to realize that it's right in the middle of a sermon about money and missions. We saw yesterday that the preceding verse is a command by our Lord to do some Gospel leveraging of our dwindling resources by spending our "unrighteous wealth" to populate heaven. And the verses after verse 10 keep talking about money until the famous climactic statement in verse 13: "You cannot serve God and money." Evidently, God thinks that a Christian and his money aren't parted soon enough.

I think the older English translations are correct in using the superlative "least" instead of "very little" in verse 10. With this word, our Lord is making a huge counter-cultural statement. He's saying that what the world says is the most important thing is actually the least important thing in this world, the bottom-dweller of priorities and values. Well, what is that? He tells us in the next verse: "If then you have not been faithful in the *unrighteous wealth*, who will entrust to you the true riches?" (v. 11, emphasis mine) Money! Wealth! Possessions! All that stuff that the world puts at #1 or #2, the Lord puts at the very bottom of the heap in importance. The Lord turns everything upside down (which means, of course, that He's turning it right side up).

To God, money is the least of all things in this world. (They use gold as paving stones in heaven, after all.) The Lord is dissing what you and I so deeply value and have such a hard time parting with. This interpretation is confirmed in verses 14 and 15: "The Pharisees, who were lovers of money, heard all these things, and they ridiculed him. And he said to them, 'You are those who justify yourselves before men, but God knows your hearts. For what is exalted among men is an abomination in the sight of God.'"

It's an "abomination in the sight of God" to take a worthless, corruptible pile of stuff—the least of the least—and elevate it as though it were something important. The word "abomination" is often used in the Bible in solemn warnings against idolatry; and warning us against idolatry is exactly what the Lord does in verse 13. Listen and fear: "No servant can serve two masters, for either he will hate the one and love the other, or he will be devoted to the one and despise the other. You cannot serve God and money."

He didn't say, "It sure is hard to serve both God and money." He said you can't do it. It's impossible. How can you serve the greatest thing and the least thing at the same time? Don't trade your life for the least valuable thing in this world: money and possessions. Instead, make your money serve you and your Gospel ambitions to make God famous all over this earth.

To me, this passage is one of the most encouraging in the Bible regarding a believer's duty to missions. Not all of us can help open Albania for Christ like Dave Hosaflook, or lead a missions organization like Tim Keesee, but every last one of us can leverage our admittedly meager resources for incredible eternal returns.

The shrewd and his money are soon parted.

Let the Gospel stir your heart to spend and be spent to help people to heaven. —JD

SOULS & GOURDS

And should not I pity Nineveh, that great city? JONAH 4:11

Jonah wasn't exactly an example of missionary fidelity. When God said to go east, he went west. When God said preach, he pouted. When God eventually coerced him to evangelize, he did so begrudgingly. Still, God used Jonah's message and saved an entire city—the greatest revival in human history. (Think of 500,000 converts from one evangelistic meeting!) So the book has a happy ending. Well, almost. Had I been asked to edit it, I probably would have suggested omitting chapter 4 altogether. Chapter 3 has a nice "feel good" conclusion. Stop right there. Run the credits. But the book continues, taking an anticlimactic turn. *Nineveh repents. God relents. Jonah resents.* Ouch. But if we read Jonah 4 with fresh eyes, we'll see a bit of ourselves as well.

Like Jonah, we're better patriots than prophets. Jonah was "displeased" that God spared the Ninevites, Israel's enemies (4:1). Exceedingly angry. "I-want-to-die" angry (4:3). He charged God with incompetence (4:2-3), throwing the great revelation of God's glory from Exodus 34:6-7 in His face as an accusation: "I tried to avoid this. I *knew* You'd be gracious and forgiving. That's *just like* You. And it's disgusting." His hatred for the Ninevites was so deep that he lashed out at God when their destruction didn't come. In a telling statement, he recalled the good old days when he was back in "*his* country" (4:2) rather than God-forsaken (he wished) Assyria. He exited the city and made himself an observatory at a safe distance (4:5): "Maybe God listened to my airtight reasoning and will destroy these pagans after all. Here's hoping."

Like Jonah, we get happy over the wrong things. Though Jonah deserved to be destroyed for his blasphemous rebellion, God instead walked him through an object lesson. He started by giving Jonah a nice plant, probably some kind of gourd (4:6). Jonah wasn't all sulk after all. For the only time in four chapters, Jonah was happy. His joy was extravagant—he was "exceedingly joyful," as he had been "exceedingly angry." What was the cause of all this mirth? A stupid plant. Now, I honestly don't relate to people who talk about the fruit of their tomato plants as if they were grandchildren. Gardening's not my thing. But I do relate to getting way too happy over inconsequential things. I'm more like Jonah than I like to admit.

> *"Sure, people are perishing every minute of the day—but what a ballgame!"*
> *"Half the world is closed to the Gospel—and have you seen the new iPhone?!"*
> *"The world is steeped in idolatry—and my yard looks great!"*

Like Jonah, we get angry over the wrong things. God's living parable wasn't finished. He sent a worm to eat the gourd and a sultry wind to make its absence felt (4:7-8). That pushed Jonah over the edge. Once again, he asked for death (4:9). "How dare God destroy my innocent plant? I loved that thing. Has He *no* pity?" His response is over-the-top, but again I can relate. What really burns me up is the "gourds" of life.

> *"Was that dent in my car really necessary, God? Don't you care?!"*
> *"Have you seen that laundry pile? My life is a wreck."*
> *"My stocks are down. Again. And love handles? Really? Thanks for nothing."*

Jonah was set up for the "moral of the story," as are we. He pitied a disposable plant he had neither made nor nurtured (4:10). If nothing else, the suddenly eco-conscious prophet should have cared for the city's cattle (4:11). Yet, he faulted God for saving a great city of people—of children!—whom God had made and who would live somewhere forever (4:11). And that's where the story ends, with God's probing question, "Should not I pity?" It's unsatisfying. But it leaves us to ponder the missionary implications of the question. *Shouldn't* God pity the lost? Shouldn't *we*?

Let the Gospel inspire you to live as though souls are more significant than gourds. —CHRIS

A WORLD OF CONFUSION

You were slain, and by your blood you ransomed people for God from every tribe and language and people and nation. REVELATION 5:9

The Tower of Babel wasn't intended to humor children with unintelligible babbling in Sunday School. It's a dark and tragic story intended to make sense of the confused diversity and godless unity of the real world around us. As Kostenberger and O'Brien have written, "By the time we arrive at Genesis 11 we have reached the nadir [lowest point] of human existence with a fractured and disastrously broken society that has lost any sense of God-centeredness" (*Salvation to the Ends of the Earth*, p. 28). Our world is comprised of billions of people, speaking thousands of languages, living in hundreds of countries. Yet, despite this diversity, there exists one pervasive, selfish, anti-God mindset (see Ephesians 2:1-3). Genesis 11 describes how we got into this mess; Genesis 12 describes God's plan to get us out of it.

Our confusion points back to our corruption. The civilization at Babel was technologically ingenious (11:3) yet self-promoting and God-defying (11:4). The great sin of Babel was not (as some think) that people were trying to get to God. They were trying to *be* God. Rather than filling the earth with the glory of God's name (9:1, 7), they wanted to magnify their own supposed greatness. The Lord *stooped* ("came down" in 11:5) to see their tall ambitions, and He effortlessly ended them. He confused the people's languages and dispersed their population (11:7-8; Acts 17:26-27). This judgment didn't change humanity's heart. Throughout Scripture, Babylon (the geographic and spiritual descendants of Babel) continually opposed God and His people (Isaiah 14, Jeremiah 50–51, Daniel 1–4). Although God's intervention at Babel didn't fix humanity's ultimate problem, it did slow down our sinful progress and delay our eventual self-destruction (11:6). Together, we were a ticking time bomb. Had God not divided our world, humanity would have exploded with corruption.

Our confusion points ahead to our redemption. Was the confusion at Babel judgment or grace? In the end, it seems that it was *all* grace. Look at God's promise to Abraham: "In you all the families of the earth will be blessed" (12:3). *All the families of the earth?* Where did *they* come from? God split humanity into pieces at Babel, then promised to bless every piece through Abraham's seed. This promise to Abraham wasn't merely a good intention; it was an eternal covenant. God has been committed to it for four millennia! Jesus Christ, "the son of Abraham" (Matthew 1:1), came "in order to confirm the promises given to the patriarchs, and in order that the Gentiles might glorify God for His mercy" (Romans 15:8-9; Luke 1:54-55). As more Gentiles put their faith in Jesus Christ, God continues to fulfill His promise to bless all peoples through Abraham and make Abraham "the father of many nations" (Galatians 3:7-16; Romans 4:16-25). In fulfillment of His promise, the Lord will see to it that the Gospel advances among every nation (Matthew 24:14). God will ensure that Gospel preaching is so effective that sinners "from every nation, from all tribes and peoples and languages" will unite once again, not in defiance of God, but in praise of Him (Revelation 5:9; 7:9-10)! In a glorious reversal of Babel's confusion, people of every language will unite their voices to worship the Lamb who saved them from corruption by His blood!

Through evangelism and missions, we take part in God's massive plan of redemption. Every time we reach an unbeliever with the Gospel, we're participating in God's sublime, certain, cosmic plan; we're both fulfilling biblical prophecy and bringing glory to Jesus. What a glorious privilege!

Let the Gospel encourage you to penetrate the world's confusion for Christ's glory. —JOE

PRAYER FOR THE PERSECUTED

Remember those who are in prison, as though in prison with them.
HEBREWS 13:3

An unexpected knock interrupted the house church meeting. The believers inside, still grieving over the death of one of their leaders, had been on their knees into the night praying for the release from prison of another one of their pastors. Then came a knock at the door in the dead of night. Was it the police, or just a stranger who had lost his way and saw a light in the window?

> And when he knocked at the door of the gateway, a servant girl named Rhoda came to answer. Recognizing Peter's voice, in her joy she did not open the gate but ran in and reported that Peter was standing at the gate. They said to her, "You are out of your mind." But she kept insisting that it was so, and they kept saying, "It is his angel!" But Peter continued knocking, and when they opened, they saw him and were amazed. (Acts 12:13-16)

Isn't it ironic that when the Lord delivered Peter out of prison that night that every door opened up before him—except the church door? This wonderful passage provides a kind of comic relief in the midst of Herod's persecution: a prayer meeting interrupted by the very answer to those prayers. And if we are very honest with ourselves, these first-century Christians seem strangely familiar—like the 21st-century variety. We pray, yes; but we usually keep our expectations low so that we won't be disappointed with the results—and we rarely are.

What does this have to do with our response to the rise in Christian persecution in our day? It is interesting that one of the first recorded prayer meetings following Pentecost finds the church on their knees on behalf of a persecuted believer. Even though their faith was small, their God was not. Hebrews 13:3 commands us to "remember those who are in prison, as though in prison with them, and those who are mistreated, since you also are in the body."

When we pray for persecuted brothers, we don't only seek their deliverance, though that's legitimate. We pray for their boldness (Acts 4:29; Ephesians 6:19-20). We pray for the further glory of Christ, something accomplished both by life and by death, from the pulpit and from the prison cell (Philippians 1:12-21). God's purposes are sometimes accomplished through suffering. A courageous Christian journalist in Turkey once told me that if human rights organizations had existed when Joseph was unjustly imprisoned in Egypt, they would have sought his immediate release. But God had a higher purpose than just delivering Joseph. God's design was not only to deliver Joseph but also to deliver *nations* (Genesis 50:20).

Of course, we don't know God's plans, but still we are to pray for and encourage persecuted Christians. As the writer of Hebrews explains, they and we are "in the body." The Gospel binds believers together worldwide. Those who are being persecuted at this very hour are our brothers and sisters through faith in Christ. They are part of His body. Just as the Lord identifies with His people in their suffering (Exodus 3:7; Acts 9:4-5), so we are to identify with them as well. If we embrace this truth, how can we remain indifferent to a family member's pain?

Even though most of us are a comfortable distance from the frontlines, we can get into the fight by getting on our knees! Pray for grace for those in harm's way. Pray for protection and peace. Pray for boldness in the Gospel so that Christ, who first suffered for us, would be magnified in and through the suffering of His people.

Let the Gospel knit your heart with the hearts of your persecuted brothers and sisters. —TIM

AGGRESSIVE, ANTIOCH-LIKE ADVANCE

Set apart for me Barnabas and Saul for the work to which I have called them.
ACTS 13:2

My favorite New Testament church, hands down, is the church at Antioch, "the true mother-church of evangelical Christianity" (Alexander Whyte). The church at Jerusalem was the hub of the early church. But, like many of our churches, it was reticent to accept the multi-ethnic implications of the Great Commission. An audacious mission required an audacious church like Antioch to lead the way.

The Antioch church was a Gospel maternity ward (11:19-20). Acts 11:19 begins with a flashback to Acts 8:4. Because of God-ordained persecution, the Gospel was finally spreading from Jerusalem, but it was running in the sand rather than making an all-out sprint. Aside from Cornelius-type exceptions (Acts 10), evangelism was still limited to "Jews only" (11:19). Typical Christians didn't preach to (gasp!) *Gentiles*. That would finally change at Antioch, where unnamed, revolutionary laymen decided to disregard precedence and introduce non-Jews to King Jesus (11:20). The risk-taking nature of those early church planters became part of the DNA of the church. God displayed His saving power (11:21, 24), and the missions movement began in earnest.

The Antioch church was a Gospel melting pot (11:21; 13:1). Antioch was an "outside-the-box" church even by today's standards. It was ethnically and socially diverse. At least one of its leaders was black—Simeon, called Niger. Another hailed from the African province of Cyrene (modern Libya)—Lucius. Still another was a relative or family friend of Herod—Manaen. The church was simultaneously cosmopolitan and Christlike (11:26b). It was living, breathing proof that the Gospel is no respecter of persons. It crosses geographical, socio-economic, and ethnic boundaries.

The Antioch church was a Gospel academy (11:22-26). The Antioch believers were mentored by the ever-encouraging, ever-hopeful Barnabas (11:22). He rejoiced in their conversions, grounded them in the truth, and urged them to cling to Christ (11:23). He recruited a co-laborer from Tarsus named Saul (11:26b). (Heard of him?) The church grew, both numerically and spiritually. Their character and conduct so reflected Christ that they were the first believers to be called "Christians" (11:26b)—a designation probably intended as a barb but received as a badge. Aggressive evangelism led to aggressive edification, which resulted in still more aggressive evangelism (11:24).

The Antioch church was a Gospel slingshot (11:27-30; 13:1-3). Antioch's influence stretched beyond home in two exemplary ways. They gave their money to needy Judean brothers (11:27-30), but that was just a start. They gave their *pastors* (13:1-3)! That's staggering. Losing Paul or Barnabas would be tough. Losing both at once—devastating! Yet, they didn't lose them, they *launched* them to reach the unreached. And the church didn't miss a beat (14:26-28; 15:35; 18:22). It's a tough lesson to learn. Pastors and missionaries are tempted to maintain white-knuckled control, as if they're irreplaceable and others incompetent. Yet, leaders of healthy churches are surprisingly expendable, evidencing truly indigenous ministry. What God did in Antioch was sustainable and reproducible. Paul and Barnabas taught faithful men (2 Timothy 2:2), then got out of the way. Augustus Strong put it this way in his *Systematic Theology*:

> That minister is most successful who gets the whole body to move, and who renders the church independent of himself. The test of his work is not while he is with them, but after he leaves them. Then it can be seen whether he has taught them to follow him, or to follow Christ; whether he has led them to … independent Christian activity, or … made them passively dependent upon himself. (p. 908)

Let the Gospel demonstrate its power through risk-taking, self-replacing ministry. —CHRIS

YONDER VILLAGE

To preach the gospel in the regions beyond you. 2 CORINTHIANS 10:16

The book of Romans is Paul's masterpiece. Swiss commentator Godet calls it "the cathedral of the Christian faith." I love that, but from the vantage point of a "pioneer" missionary, I view it more as a cathedral on wheels—the *Land Rover* of the Christian faith, if you will. The Romans Rover is stuffed with soteriological treasure, but it is designed for travel—preferably off road. The front bumper says, "Not Ashamed of the Gospel of Christ!" (1:21); the back bumper says, "Unreached Territory or Bust!" (15:20).

Again and again and again (15:9, 10, 11, 12, 21), Paul quotes Old Testament prophecy to remind us that the Gospel is for *all* people, not just Jews. He was fueled by the Scriptures, not just his Damascus Road experience. So we can't give ourselves an "I'm-not-an-apostle" pass. We have more Bible than Paul had, and it tells us that the Gospel must reach those who have never heard (15:21). Good news is meaningless until it arrives.

Jesus Himself established the new *modus operandi*. When He became famous in one place, He didn't build a cathedral and wait for the nations to notice. He moved out. He moved *on* to preach in Nexttown or Yonder Village (Mark 1:37-39, Luke 8:1). Paul embraced this pattern. After he established a church, he pulled up his stakes and moved on (Romans 15:23). Why? Because the churches were fully mature? No! Corinth alone could've used him indefinitely. He left to meet a greater need: the vast swaths of people who had no churches at all—in "the regions beyond" Paul and his churches to date (2 Corinthians 10:16). It was like Paul had voices perpetually resounding in his head—echoes of the Macedonian Call (Acts 16:9). He had already preached from Jerusalem all the way to my Illyricum (modern Albania), over 1000 miles away (Romans 15:19). But you should see what's next on Paul's "bucket list"! He's bound for Rome, the imperial capital (Romans 1:15). And even that wasn't his ultimate destination. It was merely a layover en route to the furthest reaches of the empire—Spain—"the ends of the earth" as he knew it (Romans 15:24; Acts 13:47).

Paul taught us that the essence of missions is going places where Christ is *not* already named (Romans 15:20). I don't understand why church planters so frequently ignore that little word *not*. The mission is not to plant the *coolest* church in town, but the *only* church in town. Why target The Bible Belt when so many places don't even have a Bible? Roughly 35% of the world has *no access* to the Gospel. I'm not talking about the people in your neighborhood who have never heard "a clear presentation of the Gospel" (but could if you would just cross the street). I'm talking about the 2,400,000,000 people who couldn't find a Christian if they tried. How is this possible? How many of our mission workers are even targeting them? I *might* be satisfied with a proportionate 35%. But get this: *it's less than 5%!* Tip a waitress 5% and she'll spit in your soup the next time you order lunch. Five measly percent is a yawn in the face of the Great Commission, a shrug at the plight of the damned. It's tantamount to telling the unreached to go to Hell.

Forgive my candor, but I don't know how else to verbalize what our inaction is communicating. We're cloistered in climate-controlled cathedrals, feasting while billions can't even find a drop of Water. "We do not well! This day is a day of good tidings!" (2 Kings 7:9). Our main problem isn't fear. Certainly we prefer our crosses gilded, not bloody—but there's a bigger issue. Christ is not our life (Philippians 1:21). We're self-absorbed. Distracted. Apathetic. Unimpressed at the stunning honor of fulfilling biblical prophecies. Passionate about anything other than harvest fields of unreached souls—unreached not because they're unreachable, but because we've chosen not to reach them.

The Romans Rover is warmed up and ready to roll. Jesus is driving. The ride won't be smooth. But there's a seat with your name all over it. You in?

Let the Gospel reach its target by sending and taking it where it isn't. —DAVID